**DEVELOPMENT OF PHARMACY
SERVICE WEIGHTS** in the
IMPLEMENTATION of
CASEMIX SYSTEM
for PROVIDER PAYMENT

DEVELOPMENT OF PHARMACY SERVICE WEIGHTS in the IMPLEMENTATION of CASEMIX SYSTEM for PROVIDER PAYMENT

CONCEPT, METHODS AND APPLICATIONS

DR ALJUNID
AND
DR JADOO

PARTRIDGE

Copyright © 2017 by Prof Dr Syed Mohamed Aljunid MD; MPH; PhD and Dr Saad Ahmed Ali Jadoo MBBCH; MSc; PhD.

ISBN: Softcover   978-1-5437-4291-6
         eBook   978-1-5437-4290-9

All rights reserved. No part of this book may be used or reproduced by any means, graphic, electronic, or mechanical, including photocopying, recording, taping or by any information storage retrieval system without the written permission of the author except in the case of brief quotations embodied in critical articles and reviews.

Because of the dynamic nature of the Internet, any web addresses or links contained in this book may have changed since publication and may no longer be valid. The views expressed in this work are solely those of the author and do not necessarily reflect the views of the publisher, and the publisher hereby disclaims any responsibility for them.

Print information available on the last page.

To order additional copies of this book, contact
Toll Free 800 101 2657 (Singapore)
Toll Free 1 800 81 7340 (Malaysia)
orders.singapore@partridgepublishing.com

www.partridgepublishing.com/singapore

TABLE OF CONTENTS

LIST OF TABLES ix
LIST OF FIGURES xi
ACKNOWLEDGMENT xiii
SUMMARY xv
LIST OF ABBREVIATIONS xvii

CHAPTER I: INTRODUCTION 1
  1.1   Study Background 1
  1.2   Universiti Kebangsaan Malaysia (UKM) 4
        1.2.1   University Kebangsaan Malaysia Medical
               Center (UKMMC) 5
        1.2.3   Development of Casemix System in UKMMC 6

  1.3   Pharmacy Profile in UKMMC 8
  1.4   Problem Statement 13
  1.5   Justification and Importance of the Study 14
  1.6   Conclusion 15

CHAPTER II: LITERATURE REVIEW 16
  2.1   Introduction 16
  2.2   Cost and Importance of Costing 16
  2.3   Costing Approaches 17
        2.3.11 Step-down Costing 18
        2.3.2   Bottom-Up Costing 19

  2.4   Relative Values 20
  2.5   Concept of Cost-Weights 21
  2.6   Definition of Casemix System 22
        2.6.1   History of Casemix and DRGs 23
        2.6.2   Why Casemix? 24

  2.7   Diagnosis Related Groups (DRGs) 25
  2.8   Types of DRG 26
        2.8.1   Medicare DRGs 26
        2.8.2   Refined DRGs 27

  2.8.3 All Patient-DRG (AP-DRG) 28
  2.8.4 Severity DRGs 28
  2.8.5 All Patient Refined-DRG (APR-DRG) 29
  2.8.6 International Refined-DRG (IR-DRG) 30

2.9 MY-DRG 31
2.10 Data Trimming Issue 34
2.11 Electronic Prescription System 35
2.12 Predictors of the Total Pharmacy Cost 36
2.13 Conceptual Framework 38
2.14 Research Objectives 39
  2.14.1 General objective: 39
  2.14.2 Specific objectives: 40

2.15 Hypothesis 40
2.16 Conclusion 40

CHAPTER III: METHODOLOGY 42
3.1 Introduction 42
3.2 Study Background 42
3.3 Study Design 43
3.4 Research Setting 43
3.5 Target Population 43
3.6 Sampling Method and Sample Calculation 44
3.7 Data Issues 44
  3.7.1 Step One: Identifying the Pharmacy Component ...44
  3.7.2 Step Two: Source of Data and DRG Assignment ...45
  3.7.3 Step Three: Calculation of the Total
     Pharmacy Cost 46
  3.7.3 Calculation of patient level total pharmacy costs 49
  3.7.4 Step Four: Data Trimming 49
  3.7.5 Step Five: Calculation the Pharmacy
     Service Weight per each MY-DRG 50

3.8 Inclusion and Exclusion Criteria 50
  3.8.1 Inclusion criteria for patients 50
  3.8.2 Exclusion criteria for patients 50

3.10 Ethics 51

3.11 Variables..51
    3.11.1 Dependent Variables 51
    3.11.2 Independent Variables...51

3.12 Data Analysis 51
3.13 Operational Definition..52
3.14 Conclusion...54

CHAPTER IV: RESULTS 55
4.1 Introduction..55
4.2 Descriptive Results 55
    4.2.1 Patient Level Data...55
    4.2.2 Socio Demographic and Clinical Background of Patients 56
    4.2.3 DRG Assignment..58
    4.2.4 Casemix Major Groups Assignment 58

4.3 Calculation of the Total Pharmacy Cost 60
    4.3.1 Unit Cost of the Pharmacy Use of the Overhead Cost Centers Allocation 60
    4.3.2 Unit Cost of the Pharmacy Equipment Cost (Capital Costs)..63
    4.3.3 Unit Cost of the Pharmacy Staff Serviced Inpatients...63
    4.3.4 Unit Cost of inpatient drugs/medicines and medical supplies 63
    4.3.5 Calculation of Patient Level Total Pharmacy Costs....65
    4.3.6 Total Pharmacy Cost...67

4.4 Predicting Factors Influencing the Study Outcome...........67
4.5 Descriptive Analyses 68
4.6 Study of Outliers...69
    4.6.1 Descriptive Analysis 70

4.7 Bivariate Analysis to Predict Total Pharmacy Cost 71
    4.7.1 Association Between Age of Patients and Total Pharmacy Cost..72
    4.7.2 Association Between Length of Stay and Total Pharmacy Cost..72

  4.7.3 Association Between Number of Items and Total Pharmacy Cost 72
  4.7.4 Association between Gender and Total Pharmacy Cost..73
  4.7.5 Association between Type of Cases and Total Pharmacy Cost 73
  4.7.6 Association between Ethnicity and Total Pharmacy Cost..73
  4.7.7 Association between Level of Severity and Total Pharmacy Cost 74
  4.7.8 Association between all Independent Variables and the Total Inpatient Pharmacy Cost 75

4.8 Multivariate Linear Regression Analysis............................78
  4.8.1 Regression Model Fitness 78
  4.8.2 Statistical Significance..78
  4.8.3 Estimated Model Coefficients 79
  4.8.4 Interpretation of Regression Model Equation.........79

4.9 Development of Casemix Pharmacy In-Patient Service Weights 82
4.10 Conclusion..84

CHAPTER V: DISCUSSION 87
5.1 Introduction...87
5.2 Costing Methodology..87
5.3 Predictors of the Total Inpatient Pharmacy Cost..............90
5.4 Development of Casemix Pharmacy Service Weight.........93

CHAPTER VI: CONCLUSION AND RECOMMENDATION 97
6.1 Conclusion...97
6.2 Limitation of Study..99
6.3 Recommendations...99

REFERENCES 101
APPENDIX A: PHARMACY SERVICE WEIGHTS OF 450 UTILIZED MY-DRGS 119

LIST OF TABLES

Table:	Description	
1.1	Total Pharmacy Budget Used of 2011 (Drugs only)	8
1.2	Frequency Distribution of UKMMC pharmacy staff	9
2.1	Casemix Major Group (CMG) codes and description used in MY-DRG	33
4.1	Descriptive statistics of age, length of stay, number of items and total pharmacy cost of patients (n=20,192)	57
4.2	Socio demographic and clinical characteristics of categorical variables of patients (n= 20, 192)	57
4.3	Casemix Major Groups (CMG) codes used in MY-DRG (n= 20,192)	58
4.4	Pharmacy use of the overhead cost centers and the allocation factors	62
4.5	UKMMC inpatient pharmacy staff salary, 2011 (n=20)	64
4.6	Sample of the total pharmacy cost calculation per patient /episode (n = 15 out of 20,192)	66
4.7	Inpatient pharmacy cost components (n=20,192)	67
4.8	Descriptive statistics of age, length of stay, number of items and total pharmacy cost of patients (Trimmed data, n=13,673)	68
4.9	Socio demographic and clinical characteristics of categorical variables of patients (Trimmed data, n=13,673)	69
4.10	Descriptive statistics of age, length of stay, number of items and total pharmacy cost of patients (Outliers, n= 6,519)	70
4.11	Socio demographic and clinical characteristics of categorical variables of patients (Outliers, n= 6,519)	71
4.12	Correlation between age, length of stay, number of items and total inpatient pharmacy cost (Trimmed data, n=13,673)	72

4.13	Ethnicity comparison to total pharmacy cost (ANOVA analysis of Trimmed data, n=13,673)	74
4.14	Severity level comparison to total pharmacy cost (ANOVA analysis, n=13,673)	75
4.15	Zero-order correlation between socio demographic, clinical and total pharmacy cost (n= 13.673)	77
4.16	Model summary of linear regression Model	78
4.17	ANOVA test to examine the fitness of model for (the trimmed data, n=13,673)	79
4.18	Multivariate linear regression coefficients results	82
4.19	Casemix Major Groups (CMG) codes and description used in MY-DRG (n= 13,673)	83
4.20	Pharmacy in-patient service weights of the highest 20 MY-DRGs.	85
4.21	Pharmacy in-patient service weights of the lowest 20 MY-DRGs.	86

LIST OF FIGURES

Figure:	Description	
2.1	MY-DRG with 5 digit system	32
2.2	Flow Chart of Study	39
4.1	Total pharmacy uses of twelve overhead cost centres allocation in (%).	61

ACKNOWLEDGMENT

In the name of Allah, the Most Gracious and the Most Merciful. First of all, Alhamdulillah and praise to Allah for His Grace and His Mercy in giving us the health, patience and strengths to complete this book.

We would like to extend our greatest sense of gratitude to Universiti Kebangsaan Malaysia Medical Centre, especially the International Centre for Casemix and Clinical Coding, UKM and United Nations University-International Institute for Global Health for their institutional support in conducting the research that provide all the information for this book. We would like to thank UKM Research and Ethics Committee for the approval to conduct this extensive study.

Our greatest thanks and gratitude goes to our entire families for their support and understanding in completing this book.

SUMMARY

The service weight is among several issues and challenges in the implementation of casemix in developing countries, including Malaysia. The aim of this study is to develop the Malaysian Diagnosis Related Group (MY-DRG) casemix pharmacy service weight in University Kebangsaan Malaysia-Medical Center (UKMMC) by identifying the cost of pharmacy services by each casemix groups in the hospital. All patients admitted to UKMMC in 2011 were recruited in this study. Combination of step-down and bottom-up costing methodology was used in this study. The drug and supplies cost, the cost of staff, the overhead cost and the equipment cost make up the four components of pharmacy cost. The total pharmacy cost was obtained by summing all the pharmacy components' cost per each MY-DRG. Descriptive analyses, bivariate correlation and multiple linear regression analyses were conducted to predict the total pharmacy cost from various potential predictors. A total of 13,673 patients were investigated with average age of 43.53 years (SD 22.27 years) of which 5,767 (42.2%) were males and 7,906 (57.8%) were females. Majority were Malay (49.3%), followed by Chinese (27.8%), Indian (13.8%), others (9.1%) respectively. Majority of cases were medical cases (61.9%) compared to (38.1%) as surgical cases. Most of the patients (53.6%, n=7,329) were in severity level I, 30.8% (n=4,210) patients were in severity level II and 15.6% (n=2,134 patients) were in severity level III respectively. The average length of stay is 6.76 (SD 7.16) days and median of 4 days. The total number of drugs and supplies (items) prescribed for all 13,673 patients were over 111,794 items with average of 8.18 (SD=5.81) and median of 6 items. Drugs and supplies were the main component (86.0%) of pharmacy cost compared to overhead cost (7.3%), staff cost (6.5%) and pharmacy equipments (0.2%) respectively. Out of 789 inpatient MY-DRGs casemix groups, 450 (57.0%) groups were utilized by the UKMMC. Pharmacy service weight was calculated for each of these 450 MY-DRGs groups. MY-DRG casemix group of Lymphoma & Chronic Leukemia group with severity level three (C-4-11-III) has the highest pharmacy service weight of 11.8 equivalents to average pharmacy cost of RM 5,384. While the MY-DRG casemix group for male circumcision with severity level one (V-1-15-I) has the lowest pharmacy service weight of 0.04 equivalents to average pharmacy cost of RM 18. The multivariate model with demographic and clinical variables explained 32.7% of variance in total pharmacy cost ($F_{(8, 13,664)} = 829.328$, $P < 0.0005$). Length of stay ($B = 0.349$, $P < 0.0005$) and severity level III ($B = 0.253$, $P < 0.0005$) appeared to be the strongest predictors of the total pharmacy cost; followed by the number of items ($B = 0.081$, $P < 0.0005$) and severity level II ($B = 0.050$, $P = <0.0005$). In conclusion, increase in the hospitalization period accompanied with a major complication and comorbidity had the highest influence on the total pharmacy cost. Knowing which DRG consumes the bulk of the resources would greatly support decision makers regarding budget planning of pharmacy services and patients' outcomes, and eventually will contribute in the quality of care and services improvement as well as an efficient use of resources in UKMMC.

LIST OF ABBREVIATIONS

ABC	Activity Based Costing
AP-DRGs	All Patient DRGs
APR-DRGs	All Patient Refined DRGs
CCU	Coronary Care Unit
CCs	Complication and Co morbidities
C-Hets	Caring Hospital Enterprise System
CICU	Cardiothoracic Intensive Care Unit
CM	Clinical Modification
CMG	Case-Mix Main Groups
CRW	Cardiac Rehabilitation Unit
CSSD	Central Sterile Supply Department
DRGs	Diagnosis Related Groups
ENT	Ear Nose and Throat
HCFA	Health Care Financing Administration
HIV	Human Immunodeficiency Viral Infection
HUKM	Hospital Universiti Kebangsaan Malaysia

ICU	Intensive Care Unit
INA-DRG	Indonesian Diagnosis Related Group
IR-DRG	International Refined Diagnosis Related Group
ITCC	International Casemix Center and Clinical Coding
KLIA	Kuala Lumpur International Airport
MOH	Ministry of Health
MY-DRG	Malaysian Diagnosis Related Group
NICU	Neonatal Intensive Care Unit
NYDH	Department Of Health New York
O&G	Obstetrics And Gynecology
R-DRGs	Refined DRGs
UKM	Univeriti Kebangsaan Malaysia
UKMMC	Univeriti Kebangsaan Malaysia Medical Centre
UNU-IIGH	United Nation University International Institute Of Global Health
UM	University Malaya
USM	Universiti Sains Malaysia
SDRGS	Severity DRGs
WHO	World Health Organization
CAP	Community-acquired pneumonia
ACS	Acute coronary syndromes
CRC	Cost of colorectal cancer

CHAPTER I

INTRODUCTION

1.1 STUDY BACKGROUND

The administrative practices and organizational structures of the hospitals became not compatible with steady growth of population and the need for more healthcare services at a reasonable cost and quality. More specifically, as indicators of the necessity for health system reform were the growing doubts about the efficiency of diagnostic procedures and treatments prescribed by doctors and the inequities in the costs for similar medical treatments across the hospital system.

Health reform process headed towards the adoption of methods and practices from the private sector management. In addition to new funding approaches such as casemix system and purchaser-provider split.

Casemix system is an information tool developed by Prof. Fetter and Thompson in Yale University, 1967. The initial purpose was to describe the output of hospitals and also to create a framework for monitoring both the quality of care provided and the utilization of resources (Fetter et al. 1980).

DRGs (Diagnosis Related Groups) were the first Casemix groupings developed to classify patients into classes or groups which are both clinically coherent and resource homogenous (Palmer et al. 1998). DRGs classify each patient case according to the diagnosis and other characteristics of the case, such as the patient's age, gender, case severity, co-morbidity and procedures performed (Mathauer & Wittenbecher 2012). The first 'Patient Groups' appeared in 1973, including 54 Major diagnostic Categories (MDCs) and 333 final DRGs (Mullin et al. 2002).

In 1983, HCFA (Health Care Finance Administration) developed a DRG system with 470 DRGs to finance health care provider under the U.S. social insurance scheme Medicare and Medicaid (Fischer 2000). Many countries have adapted DRGs into their own DRG classification, but they used alternative terms, although the principles behind them are similar: such as Australia (AR-DRG), Scandinavia, Germany (G-DRG), France, HRG (Healthcare Resource Groups, United Kingdom), Netherlands, MY-DRG in Malaysia and LKF in Austria (Kobel et al. 2011).

Since its appearance, DRGs have been used in a wide variety of applications, which eventually led to development of distinct versions. The most popular are Medicare DRGs, Refined DRGs, Severity DRGs, All Patient DRGs and All Patient Refined DRGs in addition to International Refined DRG (IR-DRG). The classification of refined DRGs includes differences in age, complications and co-morbidities that cause increase in costs. The Severity DRGs (S/SR-DRG) that appeared in 1994 includes a re-evaluation in the use of complications and co-morbidities.

The all patient DRGs (AP-DRGs) includes the population that does not belong to Medicare, as well as the Pediatric Diagnostic Related Groups and the Major Diagnostic Category 24 for patients infected with HIV. In the All Patient Refined DRGs (APR-DRGs) the classification describes the severity of the patients' illness. This refinement turned out to be a substantial change in the logic of grouping. All ages, complications' distinctions and co-morbidities were removed and replaced by two groups, one to describe the severity of the illness, and the other to represent the risk of mortality (Miranda & Cortez 2005).

DRGs are mainly used for acute inpatient care classification in addition to non acute inpatient care and outpatient case classification, but much less development and practice in this field. The DRGs was designed for the purpose of grouping patients into groups which are supposed to be both clinically meaningful and homogeneous in terms of resource utilization. The availability of data on the diagnosis and procedures undertaken constitutes the crucial point to begin the grouping of cases into a DRG-system (Kobel et al. 2011).

Relevant diagnoses and procedures are assigned to each admitted patient episode using a set of coding standards. This algorithm is embodied in the grouping software that is called the DRG grouper software (Aisbett et al. 2007). DRG payment system used the WHO's International Statistical Classification of Diseases, 10th Revision (ICD-10) for diagnoses, whereas procedure coding is more diverse and often country-specific.

DRG-based payment system consists of two main components, namely the patient case classification system, (i.e. the system of diagnosis related grouping). Where the DRG cases have a similar resource consumption pattern and at the same time is clinically meaningful, in other words, a case within the same DRG is economically and medically similar (Cylus and Irwin 2010; Park et al. 2007).

The second component is the payment rate setting mechanism that gives cost weights or prices to DRGs in relation to the intensity of resources used (Cylus and Irwin 2010). The payment rates reflect resource requirements for treating patients grouped into specific DRGs, expressed as cost weights in relation to a base rate, or average prices per group". In principle, the (simplified) formula for the DRG-payment is as follows: DRG-tariff = base-rate x cost-weight (x adjustment-factor). The base rate usually has a monetary value attached to it, whereas cost-weights usually are a relative measure (Cylus and Irwin 2010).

Cost-weights also known as the DRG Relative Weight or Resource Intensity are determined according to the relative use of resources related to the treatment within a certain DRG, with the average cost-weight being taken as '1'. To give an example, a patient in a DRG Weight 2.0 should (cost twice as much to treat), on average, as a patient in a DRG Weight 1.0. (James 2005).

Our proposed study focuses on DRG service weight for pharmacy component in MY-DRG in Malaysia. In fact, the Malaysian experience in this area deserves to be studied in depth.

The beginnings were when Hospital University Kebangsaan Malaysia (HUKM) being the first hospital that implemented Casemix system for inpatient management in Malaysia. The casemix unit has been established in June 2002. In HUKM, patients' medical records are coded manually after discharge based on International Classification of Disease (ICD) 10 for diagnosis and ICD 9-CM for procedures classifications respectively. In the early phase of the implementation in HUKM, the Casemix unit selected the International Refined Diagnosis related Grouper (IR-DRG, version 1.1) software to generate the casemix groups. Finally, these codes are stored in a computerized database called Caring Hospital Enterprise system (C-Hets) (Sapri et al. 2005).

In 2008, HUKM merged with the Faculty of Medicine to become the UKM Medical Centre (UKMMC). In addition to that since 9th March 2011 onwards, Malaysia Diagnosis related Grouper (MY-DRG) was developed and launched. MY-DRG is Malaysian Diagnosis Related Group, which developed to support the implementation of Case-mix in Malaysia health system. It was developed by researcher in ITCC (International Casemix Centre and Clinical Coding) (Aljunid et al. 2011). Development of local cost weights was among many challenges that faced this program since its application in 2002 (Rohaizat 2005).

1.2 UNIVERSITI KEBANGSAAN MALAYSIA (UKM)

Although the idea of establishing a national university was first mooted as far back as the early 1920, but Universiti Kebangsaan Malaysia (UKM) was formally established and first opened its doors in May 1970 to 192 undergraduate students in Jalan Pantai Baru, Kuala Lumpur, a temporary campus housing three main faculties, the Faculties of Science, Arts and Islamic Studies.

In October 1977, UKM moved to its present premises which form the main campus in Bangi. UKM Bangi Campus is 45 km from Kuala Lumpur International Airport (KLIA), 30 km from Kuala Lumpur city centre and 20 km from Putrajaya. UKM today has expanded to 13 well-established faculties, 16 institutes and 18 centers. In addition, UKM has two Health Campuses, the Kuala Lumpur Campus in Jalan Raja Muda Abdul Aziz, and the UKM Medical Centre in Cheras.

The Kuala Lumpur Campus consists of the Faculties of Allied Health, Pharmacy, Dentistry and the pre-clinical departments of the Medical Faculty. The Kuala Lumpur Campus was established in 1974. The campus in Cheras consists of the Medical Faculty, the UKM teaching Hospital and the UKM Medical Molecular Biology Institute (UMBI). The Cheras Campus was opened in 1997. Besides these campuses, UKM operates seven research stations (RS). Based on the excellence of its multi-discipline research fields for the past three decades, UUKM has been chosen as one of the four research universities in Malaysia in 2006. That position is further enhanced when national and international research organizations are placed in UKM, namely the Malaysia Genome Institute (MGI) and the International Institute of Global Health, United Nations University.

UKM is also a recipient of the Prime Minister Quality Award 2006. The award is in recognition of its excellent achievements in the fields of academic distinction and management. With these strong foundations, UKM is committed to uphold the standards achieve with its slogan, 'Inspiring Future, Nurturing Possibility'. On the January 26, 2012 the government granted the National University of Malaysia (UKM) full autonomy. The autonomy given to UKM in effect transfers decision-making powers from federal agencies and the ministry to the university (Kamaruddin 2006; UKM 2013).

1.2.1 University Kebangsaan Malaysia Medical Center (UKMMC)

University Kebangsaan Malaysia Medical Center (UKMMC) has an interlinked history with the UKM Medical Faculty. The UKM Medical Faculty was formed on 30 May 1972 in the main campus of UKM at Jalan Pantai Baru, Kuala Lumpur. After three years (1975), the MOH officially agreed to designate the Kuala Lumpur Hospital (HKL) as the teaching hospital for UKM. Support for expansion and in line with the needs of the nation caused the allocated building for Faculty of Medicine and HKL unable to fulfill the current requirements for educating, service and research. In 1990, the Faculty of Medicine decided to set up its own teaching hospital for long-term use. By 1 July 1997, HUKM was completed and started operating. It is one of the teaching hospitals in Malaysia in which the services provided include primary and tertiary levels as well as a reference hospital for other hospitals in Malaysia.

On 28 February 2008, the Deputy Chancellor of Universiti Kebangsaan Malaysia Prof. Tan Sri Dato' Dr. Sharifah Hapsah Syed Hasan Shahabudin made some requests to merge the Faculty of Medicine and HUKM to become the UKM Medical Centre: as an academic medical centre which is located in Cheras, Kuala Lumpur is to meet the needs of medical services education as well as medical research. UKMMC consists of a hospital, the Faculty of Medicine and the Institute of Medical Molecular Research (UMBI) (Kamaruddin 2006; UKM 2013).

1.2.3 Development of Casemix System in UKMMC

In the late 60s & 70s, Prof. Fetter and Thompson developed an information tool (casemix) to describe the output of hospitals and to create a framework for monitoring both the quality of care provided and the utilization of resources (Fetter et al. 1980). Casemix, at its most basic, refers to the range and types of patients (the mix of cases) treated by a hospital or other health service, i.e. It is a system that classifies patients into classes or groups which are both clinically coherent and resource homogenous.

Casemix is also used as a generic term to describe scientifically developed grouping mechanisms used to categorize patient care episodes in order to facilitate effective planning and management of healthcare. Casemix tools are grouping tools, i.e. they group data elements such as diagnoses, procedures, age, gender, discharge status, etc., They are thus wholly dependent on the availability, accuracy, completeness and timeliness of such data for successful implementation (Heavens 1999).

University Kebangsaan Malaysia Medical Center (UKMMC) is a teaching hospital provides tertiary level services. It was the first government hospital in Malaysia which has taken the initiative to implement the case-mix system for patient management and reimbursement.

It was introduced officially on 15th July 2002 as a result of research project conducted by researchers from Malaysian MOH and some public universities in 1996 (Saperi et al. 2005).

UKMMC's pioneer project, the Casemix system, is a model for patient management services for hospital around the country. The system serves as a tool for achieving good quality in clinical services by enhancing the efficiency and effectiveness of treatment services to patients and also stimulates research (Saperi et al. 2005). In UKMMC, patients' medical records are coded manually after discharge based on International Classification of Disease (ICD) 10 for diagnoses and ICD 9-CM for procedures. Finally, these codes are stored in a computerized database called Caring Hospital Enterprise system (C-Hets). The casemix unit under the management of Health Information department is the responsible side for running the casemix system in UKMMC (Saperi et al. 2005).

UKMMC has used International Refined Diagnosis related Grouper (IR-DRG) software as its patient classification previously initially, however on 9 March 2011 onwards, this was changed to Malaysia Diagnosis related Grouper (MY-DRG). MY-DRG is Malaysian Diagnosis Related Group, which developed to support the implementation of Casemix in Malaysia health system. It was developed by researcher in UNU-IIGH (United Nation University International Institute of Global Health) and ITCC (International Casemix Centre and Clinical Coding) (Aljunid et al 2011).

The codes were assigned using International Statistical Classification of Diseases and related health problems, 10th revision (ICD-10) for diagnosis code and 9th revision Clinical Modification (ICD-9 CM) for hospital procedure codes. This ICD is crucial in a way that, patient's diagnosis or procedures or other healthcare problems can be translated from words into alphanumeric or numeric codes to facilitate data storage, retrieval or data analysis (Saperi et al. 2005).

1.3 PHARMACY PROFILE IN UKMMC

The UKMMC pharmacy is in charge of pharmacy services for all in and outpatients of UKMMC. The total pharmacy budget (drugs and supplies only) of 2011 was in excess of RM 89,870,771 equivalent to USD 28,466,240 (Exchange Rate of 27th August 2014) with a 123 total number of staff and covering area of 2,187 (m^2). The UKMMC pharmacy office allocated almost 16% (RM 13, 880, 484.98) of the annual pharmacy drugs and supplies budget to inpatient services and recruiting only 16% (20 persons) of the total staff to manage and distribute inpatient services (tables 1.1, 1.2).

Table 1.1　Total Pharmacy Budget Used of 2011 (Drugs only)

No.	Pharmacy type	Cost (RM)	%
1	**In patient Pharmacy**	**13,880,485**	**15.45%**
2	In Patient Pharmacy (Patients Stayed more than 7 days	3,066,166	3.41%
3	Out Patient (Main Pharmacy)	22,700,093	25.26%
4	Out Patient Satellite (First Floor)	7,585,022	8.44%
5	Out Patient Satellite (Pediatrics /O&G and Nephrology)	7,001,927	7.79%
6	Out Patient Satellite (Family Medicine Clinics)	2,929,235	3.26%
7	Out Patient Satellite (A&E)	2,361,133	2.63%
8	Out Patient Satellite (Private Wing)	2,421,481	2.69%
9	Out Patient Satellite (Pharmacy Shop)	15,925,229	17.72%
10	Storage	12,000,000	13.35%
	Total Drug Budget	**89,870,771**	**100.00%**

Source: UKMMC Pharmacy Office (http://www.ppukm.ukm.my/farmasi/)

Table 1.2   Frequency Distribution of UKMMC pharmacy staff

No.	Staff	N	%
1	Total Pharmacy staff	123	100%
2	Outpatient pharmacy staff	103	0.84%
3	Inpatient pharmacy staff	20	**0.16%**

Source: HUKM Pharmacy office, Case-mix template 2011

Based on the concept of providing optimal individualized pharmaceutical care to patients, the pharmacy department in the hospital will focus on the practice of clinical pharmacy, Nevertheless the function of procurement and supply of drugs will continue because the rational and effective use of drugs can only be implemented with a management system of drug supply that is efficient and effective.

The Pharmacy Services included:

1) Main Outpatient Pharmacy: The largest pharmacy unit in UKMMC and also the heart of the outpatient pharmaceutical services. This pharmacy caters to patients from ground floor clinics (Orthopedic, Surgery, and Medical Clinics 1 & 2).
2) Satellite Pharmacies:

   a. First Floor Pharmacy: It caters mainly to patients from clinics on the 1st floor including Ear, Nose & Throat (ENT); Ophthalmology; Psychiatry; Maxillofacial; Endoscopy; Oncology; Citizens Clinic.
   b. Emergency Pharmacy: Its main function is to supply medications to discharged patients from the wards and also to the public who seek medical treatment at the Emergency Medicine Department.
   c. Pediatric, O&G and SLE Pharmacy (PONS Pharmacy): the second largest Outpatient Pharmacy services. The scope

of services has also been extended to patients from the Nephrology & SLE Clinic as well as repeat patients from Ward Medical 3 (6F).
d. Outpatient counseling services are made available to walk-in patients or those referred by our outpatient clinics, namely A&E, O&G, ENT, medical clinics and etc.

3) Inpatient Pharmacy: Our inpatient pharmacy is responsible for supplying medications to all wards and units in PPUKM. This department is located in the basement of the clinical block and operates daily (including public holidays). Similar to our outpatient department, all prescriptions/floor stock orders are received via online and will be screened by pharmacists or pharmacy assistants.

A systematic workflow is established within this unit to ensure efficiency when providing our services. We have also set a benchmark whereby all prescriptions are to be processed and sent to ward as early 15mins to maximum 3 hours only.

There are 4 main sub-sections located within this pharmacy:

a. Floor stock system: Our staff replenishes the floor stock trolley of wards/units on a weekly basis. Each ward/unit has a specific indent day for the week. The floor stock list of medications for each ward/unit is reviewed regularly to adjust accordingly to the usage in the wards/units.
b. Unit of use system: all prescribed medicines are supplied via in-patient name basis upon order by medical doctor. The duration of supply per order is 5 days only.
c. Dangerous Drugs (DDs) and Psychotropic: both DDs and Psychotropic items can be supplied either under the floor stock or unit of dose system based on the usage frequency of respective wards/units.

d. Manufacturing: this sub-section is in charge of producing or pre-packing of internal and external extemporaneous preparations (lotions, creams, ointments, oral solutions etc) that are not available commercially. These preparations are supplied for usage in wards/units of the hospital.

4) Total Parenteral Nutrition (TPN): This unit aims to provide and supply intravenous feeding solutions or admixtures under sterile conditions and aseptic facilities.
5) Cytotoxic Drug Reconstitution (CDR Service): this unit aims of providing safe and accurate preparation and dispensing service of injectable cytotoxic drugs to patients. The pharmacy service currently serves as a centralized reconstitution unit for the daycare, hematology, oncology, and pediatrics hematology/oncology patients at UKMMC.
6) Clinical Pharmacy Unit: there are currently 9 clinical pharmacists covering the medical wards (Medical 1-6), surgery wards (Surgery 1-7), (Coronary Care Unit (CCU), Cardiac Rehabilitation Ward (CRW), Intensive Care Unit (ICU) and Orthopedic Male and Female Wards.

This unit also started providing clinical pharmacy services to Bone Marrow Transplant ward (BMT) on part-time basis as well as accepting referrals from other wards such as Surgical, Pediatric, and Gynecology if any services are required.

7) Therapeutic Drug Monitoring (TDM) service: drugs that require TDM are those with narrow therapeutic index and potentially toxic effects such as aminoglycoside antibiotics, vancomycin, phenytoin, digoxin and theophylline.
8) Pusat Primer Tasik Selatan Pharmacy: Being the only pharmacy not within the hospital compound, it aims to serve the residents from the neighboring suburb of Bandar Tasik Selatan. It is located within a community family medical center set up by

PPUKM and is run by 4 qualified dispensers, 1 store keeper and 1 clinical attendant.
9) Drug Information Centre (DIC): Its core service is to respond to any drug-related enquiry from PPUKM hospital staff, healthcare professionals from other primary and secondary care settings, as well as the general other services provided by our DIC, which includes: Drug evaluation; active dissemination of information; providing support for drug and therapeutics committees and drug formularies; coordinating adverse drug reaction reporting scheme; providing education and training; specialist searching: using and advising on choice of primary, secondary and tertiary sources; training in drug information skills; support and advisory role and quality programme: ISO 9000:2001, MSQH, 5S.
10) Retail pharmacy was set up as an alternative source for the patients to purchase the medicines not available in the hospital formulary or to those patients not being able to get the supply from out-patient pharmacy.

As these medicines are not available in the hospital formulary & are usually propriety products, patient has to pay for the medications. The pharmacy only accepts prescriptions from PPUKM, Bandar Tasik Selatan (BTS), Klinik Kesihatan Batu 9 Cheras, and Klinik Kesihatan Batu 14 Hulu Langat. As to reduce the burden of the patient due to the high expenses in medications, PPUKM retail pharmacy also sells consignment items which have to be paid by cash term only.

11) Warfarin Clinic: the main aim of pharmacists' participation in INR clinic is to provide integrated care to the warfarin patients.
12) Quit Smoking Clinic: With the involvement of 17 pharmacists who are Certified Smoking Cessation Service Provider (CSCSP) and the use of Nicotine Replacement Therapy (NRT) and Varenicline (Champix Ò), many have benefited from this clinic.

1.4 PROBLEM STATEMENT

Many countries, including Malaysia are hindered by the lack of the availability of detailed cost of illness data, which poses a problem for pharmacoeconomic analyses relevant to the local healthcare system. Casemix and diagnosis-related groups (DRGs) system emerged in 1960s of last century compares resource utilization across groups of patients with the same principal diagnosis and can be used to provide an estimation of costs per DRG. This system was technically and clinically practical system that facilitates the estimation of patient costs, for use in pharmacoeconomic analyses (Heerey et al 2002).

The cost weight or service weight is among several issues and challenges in the implementation of casemix as a provider payment system in developing countries, including Malaysia. On the other hand, the introduction of casemix-based funding for hospitals has increased the importance in policy terms of the cost weights or the relativities on which payment rates for different patient categories are based (Jackson 2001).

Cost weights are used to estimate differences in the use of hospital resources in treating different sorts of patients. Patients in those diagnosis related groups (DRGs) assigned a high cost weight are expected, on average, to require more costly care than those assigned a low cost weight. In a prospective payment system, the cost weight is used to vary the proportion of the standard amount paid for each DRG.

Considerable research has been undertaken worldwide to estimate these relativities (Rogowski & Byrne 1990). Most research, however, has had to use data on surrogates for the cost of patient care; some using length of hospital stay, others using charges rendered for care (or charges discounted by a profit factor), and some have modeled patient care costs on the basis of care patterns and relativities from Maryland hospitals in the United States (Cotterill et al. 1986; Lave et al. 1987; Newhouse et al. 1989).

1.5 JUSTIFICATION AND IMPORTANCE OF THE STUDY

Drug costs constitute the majority of health system pharmacy budgets and continue to increase faster than other health care expenditures (Hoffman et al. 2006). It is accounting for more than 15.2 % of total health expenditure in the world in 2000 (WHO 2004) and almost a fifth of all health spending on average across OECD countries (OECD 2011). In 2006, Pharmaceutical spending ranges from a mean of (19.7% to 30.4%) in the high-income countries and the low-income countries respectively as a share of total health expenditure (Ye Lu et al. 2011).

Falkenberg and Tomson (2000) indicated that "around 50% of all medicines worldwide are prescribed, dispensed, or sold inappropriately". These inefficient and ineffective uses of medicines make it continuously a target for cost control and management evaluation (Hoffman et al. 2006).

The development of DRG in 1960s as a system comparing resource utilization across groups of patients with the same principal diagnosis greatly facilitated pharmacoeconomic evaluation (Heerey et al. 2002). The major determinant of pharmacy expenditure in any health institution is the patient complexity, so for a more effective drug costs control, methods for casemix adjustment should be considered (Aguado et al. 2008).

Today more than 40 countries worldwide implemented casemix system for various purposes and for varying levels (Saperi et al. 2005). The importance of the casemix and associated cost weights is directly proportional with the increasing demand for the development of new hospital funding methodologies in many countries.

The integrity of both the casemix grouper algorithm employed and the associated relative cost weights has a direct impact on the integrity of these new funding methodologies. While, the calculation of cost weights and the development of a casemix grouper depends on the availability of patient level case cost (Jackson 2001; Palmer et al. 1998).

UKMMC is one of the leading hospitals in Malaysia that implemented the casemix system in 2002, as an appropriated provider payment mechanism, in line with continues national health reform process towards the provision of an equitable and efficient health services. Cost weight or the service weight was among several issues and challenges that faced the implementation of casemix in Malaysia (Rohaizat, 2005). UKMMC has launched casemix program since decade ago for patient management and hospital reimbursement and recently (March 2011) developed its own MY-DRG and its related software.

As costing strategy, UKMMC applied top-down costing approach regarding the distributing of the annual budget. Thus, For the purpose of comparison the micro-costing approach (ABC) has to be carried out in detail for pharmacy services (Amrizal et al. 2005). The cost unit of the all drugs and supplies need to be known in order to detect the actual cost per patient. It has become necessary to apply this study to generate the pharmacy service weights in Malaysia by identifying pharmacy services and the actual cost of care.

It is a hope that the results of this study will participate in the development of MY-DRG in UKMMC specifically in pharmacy services by identifying which DRG consumes the bulk of the resources. So, this can greatly support decision maker regarding budget planning of pharmacy services and patients' outcomes, and eventually will contribute in the quality of care and services improvement as well as an effective use of resources.

1.6 CONCLUSION

Drug costs constitute the majority of health system pharmacy budgets and continue to increase faster than other health care. The major determinant of pharmacy expenditure in any health institution is the patient complexity, so for a more effective drug costs control, methods for casemix and DRG adjustment should be considered. Casemix and DRG systems are comparing resource utilization across groups of patients with the same principal diagnosis which greatly facilitated pharmacoeconomic evaluation in healthcare institutions.

CHAPTER II

LITERATURE REVIEW

2.1 INTRODUCTION

In this literature review section, two common types of costing methodology used in health services and in this study as well have been highlighted. Following that, it also contains about Casemix, Diagnosis Related Group and its types, objectives and hypotheses of the study.

2.2 COST AND IMPORTANCE OF COSTING

Cost is the resources spent to generate the benefits and generally considered a more valid estimate of resources Utilized (Luce et al. 1996; Munoz et al. 1989; Wagner et al. 1983). Resources may be in the form of money, time, labour or other resources used to produce a product such as health services (Luce et al. 1996; Finkler 1983).

It also can be defined either in terms of economic cost or accounting cost. Economic cost is the actual price paid by the healthcare institution for resources expended (Munoz et al. 1989).

However, the calculation of actual costs is not easy issue and commonly it is based on best estimates and averages across the hospital system. It was noted that during the implementation of casemix based payment systems the attention was focused on the coding and generation of accurate and comprehensive DRG activity data (Luce et al. 1996).

This interest is mainly because the methodologies analyzing activity patterns are well established and standards for DRG classification and coding are well documented, as well as the accurate patient's records that have been properly coded into grouper make the casemix data quite acceptable for the purpose of defining hospital production. Thus, the costing of hospital services is often neglected unintentionally (Langenbrunner et al. 2009).

The price is different to cost, but without the understanding of costs, pricing is not possible. If prices are difficult to set, then payment models that fairly pay for what hospitals produce cannot be formulated (Luce et al. 1996; Langenbrunner et al. 2009).

2.3 COSTING APPROACHES

Although International literature indicated that there are several approaches to estimate the cost of providing services by health related institution including hospitals. However, there is no unique, appropriate and acceptable methodology for costing hospital services (Mogyorosy & Smith 2005).

Type of the service and reason for costing in addition to economical feasibility of cost calculation are the main determinants for selection of appropriate costing approach. Thus, the cost of a particular service can vary substantially according to the purpose of cost data for which it was generated (Zimmerman 2003). In order to estimate the total costs of a particular health service, it is important to identify all the relevant costs, and those who bear these costs (Drummond et al. 2005; Elliott & Payne 2005).

Generally, there are three major direct cost measurement approaches: the top down, the bottom-up and the mixed approach. Although in practice gross-costing (or a top-down approach) is used most often, these techniques are frequently used simultaneously or jointly. The advantages and disadvantages of the above three methods have been widely recognized and documented (Brouwer et al.2001; Petitti 2000).

2.3.11 Step-down Costing

Basically, the step-down costing approach used to accurately detect the cost of intended results or output of the program. This is usually done by first calculating the total costs of running a hospital, then disaggregates the total costs to the department or the units of services (or products) which providing the final output of the hospital (inpatient wards and outpatient department).

Normally starts (at the top) with total expenditures and then divides these by a measure of total output (e.g. patient visits, days or admissions) to give an "average" cost per patient per visit, per day or per admission (Creese & Parker 1994). This means that all indirect costs, including overhead (administration) and support, are allocated to health care departments (cost centers), so that the full cost of providing each type of services is computed.

These indirect costs are first tracked in separate cost centers: overhead cost centre (General services) and ancillary or intermediate cost centre (Diagnostic and departmental support). Then allocate (overhead and intermediate) costs to the final cost centers ("end point of production") using an appropriate allocation unit to measure the proportion of services provided by each department (Thompson et al. 1979). The top-down approach is cheaper and faster than a bottom up approach for a number of reasons (i.e. less data intensive, fewer research skills needed and data can be collected from routine resources) and thus it is more popular (Berman et al. 1989). It can be more comprehensive (including all the relevant costs) than micro-costing. Sometimes it is the only feasible option when detailed (patient level) data is not complete (Beecham 1995; Muennig & Kahn 2002; Street & Dawson 2002; Waters & Hussey 2004).

However, because it doesn't differentiate patients with different diagnosis at the same ward and often give only a rough picture of the actual cost of patient with a specific diagnosis, so its accuracy can suffer. As a result, top-down cost estimates could overestimate unit costs if more services are provided than expected or reported (assuming that semi-fixed costs remain constant).

Conversely, it could underestimate the unit costs, if fewer services are provided than expected or reported. Moreover, it is cost estimation, and standard cost cannot be calculated this way (Edbrooke et al. 1999; Bailey 1997; Gyldmark 1995; Lievens et al. 2003). The top down approach used frequently to calculate hospital treatment costs in several countries, including Australia, Belgium, Sweden, the UK, and the USA (Jegers et al. 2002; Street 2002).

A special version of the top-down costing method, the so-called Cost Block Method, has been used to compare intensive care unit costs between hospitals and between countries (Edbrooke et al. 1999; Jegers et al. 2002; Csomos et al. 2005). Moreover, another form of top down approach is used to cost pathology services in the UK and Australia (Bailey 1997).

2.3.2 Bottom-Up Costing

The concept of bottom-up or activity based costing (ABC) was initially introduced in the manufacturing sector during 1970s and 1980s in United State. This approach was devised to resolve the shortcomings of the traditional cost accounting system regarding its inability to determine accurately the actual costs of processes (Narong, 2009).

ABC using representative samples of a particular service (and/or patient) (Evers et al. 2004; Gyldmark 1995) to record resource utilization at the patient or individual service level, and aggregates patient / service level utilization data to identify the type of resources used and to measure resource utilization in order to calculate the costs of specific services. Either retrospectively or prospectively medical records, surveys, questionnaires and other reliable databases can be employed to process the activity based costing approach (Gyldmark 1995; Jegers et al. 2002; Muennig & Kahn 2002).

The bottom-up approach is also called micro-costing. It can also be used to calculate standard costs per service and to calculate hospital costs (Bailey 1997; Negrini et al. 2004; Orlewska & Mierzejewski

2003). The micro-costing approach is more comprehensive and accurate than top down approach (macro costing).

It is also more suitable for non-homogenous services compare to top down approach (Beck et al. 1999; Edbrooke et al. 1999; Gyldmark 1995; Waters & Hussey 2004.). However, It can be very time consuming and costly, especially when applied to complex services. Generalisability can be limited. Medical records and/or resource use registration could also be inaccurate. Unit cost of resources consumed may not be available.

As it has been stated by Gyldmark (1995) and Luce et al. (1996) "the major steps in the bottom up approach may include the following:

a. Identification of activities which have a cause-and-effect relationship with the service for which the study would like to calculate costs.
b. Detailed description / identification of elements of the particular activity (resources used to deliver a service or part of the service).
c. Estimation / measurement of quantities of each element needed to undertake the activity.
d. Data can be obtained from central financing departments or databases, using cost accounting information, (electronic) medical records, etc.
e. Identification of unit costs of the elements.
f. Allocating fixed costs / overheads.
g. Calculation of the unit cost of the service in question by aggregating the costs of all the elements (activities)".

2.4 RELATIVE VALUES

The relative value unit system (RVU) can be seen as a special application of micro-costing. RVU is based on (a) the complexity of procedures, (b) the amount of resources consumed and (c) the time spent delivering the service (treatment).

One of the advantages of the RVU system is that it uses clinical activities (treatments, interventions) rather than reimbursement categories as bases for determining service level costs. On the other hand, the RVU approach assumes that each RVU consumes the same amount and the same mix of resources (West et al. 1996).

2.5 CONCEPT OF COST-WEIGHTS

Relative weights are an important component of prospective payment system, since they provide the variation in payment levels that reflect the relative resources required for visits within each classification group. The availability of cost weight enables a comparison is made between the treatment cost of various DRG cases within and between hospitals (James 2005). For the purpose of using DRG as a base of hospital payment, a price needs to be assigned to each DRG. This is usually done by assigning a cost relativity (or cost weight) with a base price multiplier (Langenbrunner et al. 2009).

The actual relative weights are unit less numbers that express the expected cost for one visit in relation to average visit. The best way to calculate relative weights is to use actual cost per inpatient case by assigning each DRG a relative value that reflects the cost of any one, or all, of the resources consumed (e.g. bed-days, theatre time, drugs, diagnostic procedures, physiotherapy and nursing treatment) in that respective DRG when compared with all DRGs (Heslop 2012).

The DRG weight for utilization of that resource is simply a ratio that compares the average resource utilization within a given DRG with the average resource utilization by all patients for all DRGs (Langenbrunner et al 2009).

Cost Weight = Average resource consumption per DRG / Average resource consumption for all cases

Cost weights also known as the DRG Relative Weight or Resource Intensity Weight (RIW) is a key to providing the costs associated with DRGs. They refer to the relative costliness of one DRG compared with another.

For example, "in a case-mix model, DRG 143 (hypertension) has a RIW of 0.5330, whilst DRG 392 (appendectomy >17 years) has a RIW of 2.846. This indicates that according to the DRG classification system, a hospital stay for hypertension is 5.3 times less costly than a hospital stay for appendectomy (Casemix Unit 1999).

The monetary value assigned to the average RIW (i.e., RIW of 1) changes annually and across countries, based on the expenditure data provided to update the case-mix model, each year (Heerey et al 2002). The data used to calculate these relative weights are the key issue. The accuracy of calculated cost weight related to the accuracy and completeness of costing data (Botz et al. 2006).

In addition to data, adjustments may be needed to ensure that the weights are an accurate measure of expected resources use. This is especially true for low volume categories since the weight for DRGs may not accurately reflect expected resources use (James 2005).

2.6 DEFINITION OF CASEMIX SYSTEM

Casemix is a broad term refers to a mix of patients classified in some way. It described a system which groups patients by predetermined factors into clinically meaningful and resource homogenous groups to describe the hospital or service product (a measure of output) (Hovenga 1996).

Casemix, at its most basic, refers to the range and types of patients (the mix of cases) treated by a hospital or other health service, i.e. It is a system that classifies patients into classes or groups which are both clinically coherent and resource homogenous (Heavens 1999). Casemix is also used as a generic term to describe scientifically developed grouping mechanisms used to categorize patient care episodes in order to facilitate effective planning, benchmarking, managing and funding health care services (Bridges et al.1999). Casemix is also referring to the tools and information systems used as a grouping tools, i.e. they group data elements such as diagnoses, procedures, age, gender, discharge status, etc., They are thus wholly dependent on the availability, accuracy, completeness and timeliness of such data for successful implementation (Heavens 1999; Clinical casemix handbook 2011-2012). Taking into account that the basic principles underlying the development of any such groupings are that they should be: clinically meaningful; resource homogeneous; limited to a manageable number of groups and derived from routinely collected data.

Casemix is underpinned by classification systems that allow meaningful comparisons of workload or throughput between facilities. The defining features of these systems are:

a. Clinical meaning. Patients in each class of the classification system should be clinically similar.
b. Resource homogeneity. Patients in each class of the classification system should utilize similar levels of resources.
c. Manageable number of classes.

The number of classes in the classification system should be large enough to ensure that the classes are clinically meaningful and resource homogenous, yet small enough to contain an adequate number of observations in each class for comparison purposes and statistical robustness (Bridges et al.1999).

2.6.1 History of Casemix and DRGs

The idea of casemix classification was dated back to middle of 19th century. Fetter (1999) believed that patients can be group according to illness, and patterns of treatment if the cases are categorized. In the beginning of 20th century a simple attempt to define the product of a hospital and describe the benefits available belonged to Dr. Codman E. a surgeon at Massachusetts General Hospital (Fetter 1991).

However the formal developments in Casemix happened in the 1960s at Oxford University. Professor Martin Feldstein discovered that the types of patients treated by a hospital (that is, the mix of services offered by the facility, for example; medicine, surgery, obstetrics and pediatrics) had a large influence on its costs. This work was continued at Yale University from about 1967 by Professor Robert Fetter, Professor John Thompson and colleagues.

The Yale group was responsible for the development of the first DRGs, and for creating a better understanding of the issues and concepts associated with Casemix. There was a demand in the 1960s for a system that enabled hospitals to identify cases that appeared to deviate considerably from the norm in respect of resource utilization and costs. DRGs were developed with this in mind (Bridges et al. 1999).

The first 'Patient Groups' or what became the DRG system was appeared in 1973, including 54 Major diagnostic Categories (MDCs) and 333 final DRGs (Mullin et al. 2002). The second version was developed for the Federal Social Security Administration and comprised 83 MDCs and 383 DRGs using ICD-8. (Fetter et al., 1980), while the third version in 1978 was developed for the State of New Jersey, which was used DRGs as a basis of a Prospective Payment System in which hospitals were paid a fixed DRGs specific amount for each patient treated. In early 1982, a much revised set of 467 categories was issued based on ICD-9 and ICD-9CM.

The final (original) version of the DRG system was developed by the Health Systems Management Group at Yale University within the framework of a contract with the Health Care Financing Administration (HCFA) to finance health care provider under the U.S. social insurance scheme Medicare and Medicaid (Fischer, 2000). HCFA-DRG system at that time comprised 470 groups across 23 MDCs. HCFA has continued to fund the development of new versions of DRGs (Rodrigues 1993; Busse et al. 2011).

2.6.2 Why Casemix?

In the beginning of the 1970s of the last century, healthcare managers in most countries of the world regardless of its classification (developed or developing countries) have begun to realize that traditional, purely financial and supply focused approaches to healthcare care management are ineffectual. In addition, hospitals or health systems produce vast quantities of heterogeneous data which cannot provide useful information without being reduced to a manageable number of categories. Addressing these issues requires the linkage of clinical and financial data using a developed information technology (IT) (Fetter 1993).

Casemix groupings are mechanisms developed in various healthcare management environments to address this requirement, and therefore are essential tools for healthcare managers. Casemix is a classification of the set, goods and services used in diagnosis, treatment and care of patient of particular clinical types. It is a classification and a measure of product of output of hospital (Palmer & Hindle 2000).

Casemix is a classification system for diseases which combined types of diseases treated in a hospital in relation with the health service expenses. Both of the hospital and its patients may benefit of the casemix implementation. Casemix is used to measure hospital output, resources allocation such as managing human resources and budget arrangement to avoid unwisely expenses, payment and fares, improvement of service quality, comparison analysis and service monitoring from time to time to ensure optimum treatment and care provided to the patient according to the level of severity (UKMMC 2002).

2.7 DIAGNOSIS RELATED GROUPS (DRGS)

The first DRG system has been developed at Yale University (Yale DRG) by Robert Fetter and his colleagues and introduced in the late 1970s. It has been used to describe acute hospital workload in more than 40 countries worldwide including USA, Australia, Canada, France and most of the west European countries in addition to some of Asian countries such as Singapore, Thailand, Japan and Malaysia (Amrizal et al. 2005). All the consequently developed DRGs have a connection to the original (Yale DRG) system (Fetter et al. 1980; Fetter 1999).

Although it was initially designed as a tool to measure hospital resource utilization, however, the hospital administration soon discovered its importance in the assessment of hospital production. The Health Care Financing Administration (HCFA) in the United States adapted the system for the purpose of monitoring and reimbursing hospital care delivered to elderly patients insured under Medicare (the federal tax-funded old-age insurance in the United States) (Fischer 1997; Chilingerian 2008).

Diagnosis-related group (DRG) systems are patient classification system (PCS). The idea of any patient classification system is to combine the confusingly large number of different patients, all appearing to be unique, into a limited number of groups with roughly similar features. Diagnosis-related group (DRG) systems have four main characteristics: (1) routinely collected data on patient discharge are used to classify patients into (2) a manageable number of groups that are (3) clinically meaningful and (4) economically homogeneous (Fetter et al. 1980; Fetter 1999).

2.8 TYPES OF DRG

The DRGS that were originally developed in the united states, which have been implemented throughout the world in different versions, have been going through a process of evolution for the last three decades; these can be grouped in five main classes: Medicare DRGs, Refined DRGs, Severity DRGs, All Patient DRGs and All Patient Refined DRGs in addition To International Refined DRG.

2.8.1 Medicare DRGs

DRGs were developed at Yale university for the US federally funded Medicare programme. It has been used as the basis of an inpatient classification system. In October 1983; Medicare lunched its DRG based prospective payment system. By the subsequent years, the responsibility for the maintenance and modification of the DRG definitions became the responsibility of the Health Care Financing Administration (HCFA).

HCFA updates the Medicare DRGs on an annual basis with focusing on problems relating primarily to the elderly population.

It has been recognized that they are deficient in a number of areas if they are to be used for the general population, e.g. Pediatrics, Obstetrics, etc. Thus there was a need in the USA to develop other Case-mix tools that addressed these deficiencies (Averill et al. 1995).

2.8.2 Refined DRGs

The HFCA-DRG system considered a complications and co morbidities (CC) as a secondary diagnosis when it causes a significant increase in hospital resource use. Few years after implementation of Medicare PPS, HFCA discovered that depending on the presence or absence of (CC) a different Medicare DRG is assigned for certain types of patients (Averill et al. 1998).

This prompted HFCA to fund a project at Yale University during the mid-1980's to help address this issue and refine the DRG methodology (Freeman et al. 1995). All CC-related diagnoses have been mapped into136 secondary diagnosis groups. Yale project identified four disease and procedure specific CC complexity levels: non-CC, moderate-CC, major-CC and catastrophic CC.

Each secondary diagnosis group was assigned to one of these levels no matter it was medical or surgical case with the exception of moderate-CC for medical cases (Averill et al. 1998; Freeman et al. 1995). If several CC were listed, the refined-DRG (R-DRG) grouper took the highest-level secondary diagnosis. The presence of multiple CC at one level did not result in grouping to a higher-level subgroup. All age and CC splits from the original DRG system were removed and replaced with these medical/surgical subgroups. Although CMS (formerly HCFA) never adopted the refined DRG system in its entirety, they did incorporate disease and procedure specific CCs in subsequent DRG revisions The DRG system developed by the Yale project is referred to as Refined DRGs or RDRGs (Miranda & Cortez 2005).

2.8.3 All Patient-DRG (AP-DRG)

The considerable success of HFCA using the Medicare DRG as PPS made them thinking about the use of DRG system as PPS for all non-Medicare patients. In 1987, The New York Health Department (NYHD studied the possibility of the application of HCFA-DRG system for a non-Medicare population and specifically for neonates and those infected with HIV.

The NYHD concluded that the HCFA-DRG system was not adequate for the non-Medicare population nor were there any provisions for the neonate or HIV infected populations (Averill et al 1998). As a result, the New York State Department of Health (NYSDH) contracted a commercial organization, 3M Health Information Systems (3M HIS) to modify the HFCA-DRG system for the non-Medicare population (Averill et al. 1998; Heavens 1999).

The changes incorporated into this new version of the DRGs included: The Pediatric Modified Diagnosis Related Groups (PM-DRG) developed by the National Association of Children's Hospitals and Related Institutions (NACHRI) has been modified and included; Introduction of Major Diagnostic Category (MDC 24) for HIV infection patients; Major CCs used as a proxy for severity; and (MDC 25) was added to capture multiple traumas. In addition, modifications were added for acute leukemia, hemophilia and sickle cell anemia, transplants, cystic fibrosis, long-term mechanical ventilation, nutritional disorders and high-risk obstetric care (Averill et al. 1998; Heavens 1999).

2.8.4 Severity DRGs

In 1993, Centers for Medicare and Medicaid Services (CMS, formerly the Health Care Financing Administration or HCFA) conducted a reevaluation of the use of complications and co morbidities within the Medicare DRGs (Federal Register 1994). This evaluation carried out for each individual diagnosis independently instead of aggregated secondary diagnosis groups. Unlike the Refined DRGs Both non-CCs and CCs were evaluated. The DRGs associated with pregnancy, newborns and pediatric patients are excluded. The major CC list from the AP-DRGs was used to identify an initial list of major CCs. Using Medicare data the categorization of each secondary diagnosis as a non-CC; non major CC or a major CC was reevaluated. The end result was that 111 diagnoses that were non-CCs in the Medicare DRGs were made a CC, 220 diagnoses that were a CC were made a non-CC and 395 CCs were considered a major CC. All CC splits in the Medicare DRGs were eliminated plus an additional 24 Medicare DRGs were merged together (Averill et al. 1998).

The resulting base DRGs were then subdivided into three, two or no subgroups based on an analysis of Medicare data. The result was 84 DRGs with no subgroups, 124 with two subgroups and 85 with three subgroups. This plus the 63 DRGs not evaluated resulted in a total of 652 SDRGs. In SDRGs, a patient is assigned to a subgroup corresponding to the highest level secondary diagnosis. Like RDRGs, multiple secondary diagnoses at a one level do not cause a patient to be assigned to a higher subgroup.

The categorization of a diagnosis as non-CC, non major CC or major CC is uniform across the SDRGs and there are no modifications for specific SDRGs. HCFA published the SDRGs in 1994, but did not establish an implementation date. The SDRGs have not been updated by HCFA since the original 1994 release (Averill et al. 1998).

2.8.5 All Patient Refined-DRG (APR-DRG)

The All Patient Refined Diagnosis Related Groups (APR-DRG) are proprietary to 3M Health Information System (HIS) (3M 1995). It's widely used throughout the United States, Europe and selected parts of Asia. They were designed specifically to address: Severity of illness; Risk of mortality; Resource intensity (Heavens 1999).

3M HIS had consecutive actions: first, is using the AP-DRGs to create so called base APR-DRGs by recombining AP-DRGs splits (removing all age and CC distinctions) and replace it by two groups: one to describe severity of illness, and the other to describe the risk of mortality, in addition to consolidating various other AP-DRGs together with some reassignment of diagnoses and procedures amongst the base DRGs (Averill et al. 1998).

Second action was the enhancement of these base APR-DRGs by adding of four 'Severity of Illness' and 'Risk of Mortality' subclasses within each base DRG (3M, 1995). Now both the severity and mortality groups contained four subgroups or subclasses which are Minor, Moderate, Major or Extreme. They are allocated according to sophisticated clinical algorithms that simultaneously evaluate multiple CCs, age, procedures and principal diagnosis. It has been shown that these algorithms ensure that patients allocated to these subclasses experience similar resource utilization and outcomes.

With these actions, a case was now assigned three distinct descriptors: i) the base-DRG; ii) the severity of illness subgroup; and iii) the risk of mortality subgroup (Averill et al. 1998). Subgroup assignment is based on interaction between secondary diagnoses, age, principal diagnosis, and the presence of certain non-operative procedures. Some non-CC in previous DRG systems were now moderate-, major- or extreme-CC or vice-versa, and multiple CC were now recognized. In addition, a completely new set of DRG was developed for the neonatal MDC (Averill et al. 1998).

2.8.6 International Refined-DRG (IR-DRG)

In response to international community demand to develop their own country-specific grouper, 3M HIS constructed the International Refined Diagnosis Related Groups (IR-DRG) using the same logic and structure as the AP-DRG and APR-DRG systems in the United State (Berlinguet et al. 2007).

The same severity of illness adjustment was included using secondary diagnoses, but only uses three subgroups: without CC, with CC and with major-CC (Mullin et al. 2002) taking into account that most international datasets do not contain more than two secondary diagnoses (Mullin et al. 2002). In addition, several DRGs eliminated from U.S. versions of the DRG system were added to capture those outpatient procedures in the U.S. that are still being performed in the inpatient setting in other countries (Mullin et al. 2002).

The underlying coding classification system was the most distinctive feature of the IR-DRG system. International grouper clearly indicated that the ICD-10 coding system would require changes in the base DRGs, depending on specific ICD-9-CM codes not available in ICD-10. Thus, IR-DRGs were modified to be compatible with both ICD-9-CM and ICD-10 (Berlinguet et al. 2007).

Therefore, at least theoretically, the new system would assure a given patient will fall in the same IR-DRG independently of the coding system used. As a result, the IR-DRG system could accommodate country-specific coding modifications and procedure coding systems. IR-DRG Version 2.0 is currently under development, and will be procedure driven in order to group all types of inpatients and outpatients (Mullin et al. 2003).

2.9 MY-DRG

Many countries have adapted DRGs into their own DRG classification, but they used alternative terms, although the principles behind them are similar: such as Australia (AR-DRG), Germany (G-DRG), France, HRG (Healthcare Resource Groups, United Kingdom), Netherlands, and LKF in Austria (Kobel et al. 2011).

Malaysian Diagnosis Related Group (MY-DRG) was successfully developed by Casemix team in UKM-International Centre for Casemix and Clinical Coding and United Nations University-International Institute for Global Health. MY-DRG characterized by its grouper.

MY-DRG grouper contains 32 CMG (Casemix Major Groups) which distributed as follows: 22 CMGs refer to Acute Care CMGs, two ambulatory CMGs, two Sub-Acute and Chronic CMGs, five Special CMGs and one Error CMGs. MY-DRG also contains maximum of 1,220 groups called CBGs (Case-Based Groups).

Each MY-DRG group was organized in 5 alpha-numeric code (one letter and four numbers):

a. First digit refers to CMG (Casemix Main Groups). CMGs are the first level of classifications labeled in Alphabet (A to Z). It mostly equivalent to chapters in ICD-10 and correspond to body systems and payment package.
b. Second digit refers to Case-Type to identify patient's type. Currently UKMMC implemented 24 CMGs inclusive 1 error.
c. Third and Fourth Digit refer to specific DRG called CBG.
d. Fifth digit, in Roman characters, refers to severity level and resource intensity level for specific package, figure 1.

Also, the MY-DRG includes three additional software applications to facilitate the implementation of the Casemix system. The Data Tool Pro is coding software. In order to facilitate coding process both of the ICD 10 and ICD 9-CM for disease and procedure classification respectively were embedded in this software. The grouping software is UNU-Grouper. This grouper converts all the diagnosis (ICD 10) and procedure (ICD 9-CM) codes into one single group called "MY-DRG. The Clinical Cost Modeling (CCM) software is costing software, consists of three modules that are: CCM module, Casemix module and Hospital Tariff module.

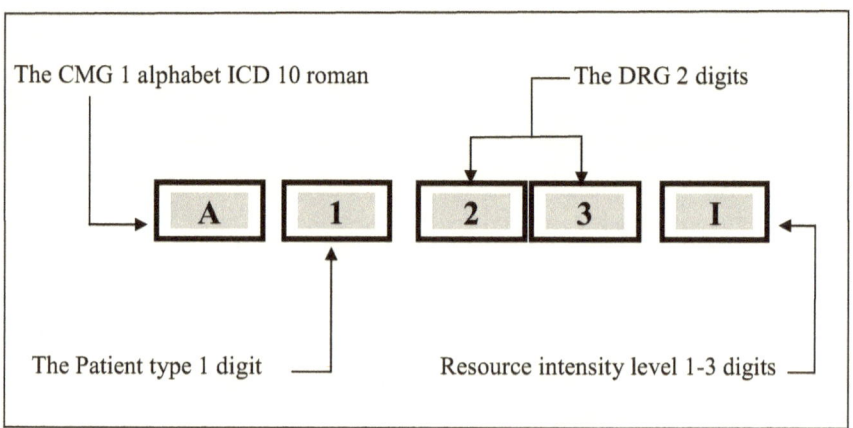

FIGURE 2.1 MY-DRG with 5 digit system

Source: International Centre for Casemix and Clinical coding, 2011

Table 2.1 Casemix Major Group (CMG) codes and description used in MY-DRG

No.	CMG codes	Description
1.	G	Central Nervous System Groups
2.	H	Eye & Adnexa Groups
3.	U	Ear, Nose, Mouth & Throat Groups
4.	J	Respiratory System Groups
5.	I	Cardiovascular System Groups
6.	K	Digestive System Groups
7.	B	Hepatobiliary & Pancreatic System Groups
8.	M	Musculoskeletal System & Connective Tissue Groups
9.	L	Skin, Subcutaneous Tissue & Breast Groups
10.	E	Endocrine System, Nutrition & Metabolism Groups
11.	N	Nephro-Urinary System Groups
12.	V	Male Reproductive System Groups
13.	W	Female Reproductive System Groups
14.	O	Deliveries Groups
15.	P	Newborns & Neonates Groups
16.	D	Haemopoeitic & Immune System Groups
17.	C	Myeloproliferative System & Neoplasms Groups
18.	A	Infectious & Parasitic Diseases Groups
19.	F	Mental Health & Behavioral Groups
20.	T	Substance Abuse & Dependence Groups
21.	S	Injuries, Poisonings & Toxic Effects Of Drugs Groups
22.	Z	Factors Influencing Health Status & Other Contacts With Health Services Groups
23.	Q	Ambulatory Groups-Episodic
24.	QP	Ambulatory Groups-Package
25.	SA	Sub-Acute Groups
26.	YY	Special Procedures
27.	DD	Special Drugs
28.	II	Special Investigations I

29	IJ	Special Investigations II
30.	RR	Special Prosthesis
31.	CD	Chronic Groups
32.	X	Errors CMGs

Source: International centre for casemix and clinical coding, 2011

2.10 DATA TRIMMING ISSUE

The DRG classification system has been developed to describe the normal, or typical, case in a DRG, known as inliers. Outlier cases are those which do not fit the normal pattern and, in terms of distribution, lie outside so called "trim points". Trimming is a method used to eliminate unusual, incorrect or otherwise conspicuous patient groups from the length of stay and average cost analysis. Trimmed data presents results after unusual value (outlier) has been removed by a trimming algorithm process (Duckett 1998). In the development of DRGs, traditional methods derived from 'exploratory data analysis' approaches have been used to define outliers, such as:

a. Inter Quartile Ranges (IQR) trimming formula: the outlier trim points were defined as follows:

Low trim point = $Q_1 - 1.5 (Q_3 - Q_1)$.
High trim point = $1.5 (Q_3 - Q_1) + Q_3$.

Where Q1 refers to the first quartile range (the first 25% of all cases) and Q3 refers to the third quartile range (the first 75% of all cases).

b. L3H3 (Lower 3, higher 3): This method mainly consists of using the average length of stay divided by three as the low trim point and the average length of stay multiplied by three as the high trim point.

Low stay trim point for DRG_1 – 1/3 average length of stay for DRG_1.

High stay trim point for DRG_1 = 3 X average length of stay for DRG_1.

c. Another approach to trimming involves setting the trim at a specified number of standard deviations above and below the mean (e.g. logarithmic conversion and trimming point at the mean + SDs).
d. Alternatively a specified percentage of the patients with highest values of the variable being analyzed and the lowest values of the variable being analyzed 9e.g. low outliers are defined as the lowest 0.5% of patient in each DRG and high outliers the highest 1%).
e. LαHα method (L alpha H alpha): The "LαHα" method is derived from the "L3H3" method. Alpha value will depend on the distribution of observations within each DRG. If they are dispersed, α will have a large value; if close, α will be small (the value of α varies from one DRG to another).

Different methods of trimming would result in a different number of patients being trimmed. Nevertheless, trimming a fixed amount of the data or only the outliers, the effectiveness of trimming depends on the criteria we adopt and the goals that we hope to achieve (APDRG Suisse 2003). In this study only L3H3 was selected as trimming formula, For example, analysis of trimmed DRG data would involve prior removal of inpatients that were in hospital with unusual low or high pharmacy cost.

2.11 ELECTRONIC PRESCRIPTION SYSTEM

E-prescribing has been defined as the process of computer-based electronic generation, transmission, and filling of a prescription, taking the place of paper and faxed prescriptions (eHealth Initiative and Center for Improving Medication Management 2008).

However, Miller & Gardner (1997) referred that the Electronic prescribing systems represent only one genre of electronic health record system activity (others include departmental pharmacy, radiology, and laboratory systems and systems for record keeping, ordering, results display, monitoring, and decision support). Because E-prescribing system allowed prescribers to electronically send patients' prescription information to pharmacy computers.

This process has decreased prescribing and medication errors and has resulted in fewer call-backs from pharmacies to physicians for clarification (Thomas et al 2012). Electronically sending and receiving prescriptions has streamlined the clinical practice workflow, and patient satisfaction and compliance have increased (Thomas et al 2012).

Additionally, connecting physician and pharmacy systems has reduced paperwork and the associated mistakes that may occur from reliance on handwritten notes (Bigler 2012). This change has produced time and cost savings for all parties involved. Fischer et al. (2008) indicated that the Clinicians who were using e-prescribing were significantly more likely to prescribe generic medications, and the potential financial savings were substantial. The more types of data and workflow are combined together in a single system or interoperable set of systems the more likely healthcare professionals can transform the benefits provided by technology into tangible improvements to patient care and organizational efficiencies (Teich 2005).

2.12 PREDICTORS OF THE TOTAL PHARMACY COST

Increasing concern over the growing share of pharmacy cost and drug expenditures as a portion of the total hospital health care over the past several years has generated a broad measures to study and control costs. Mixed factors are most likely to influence the overall drug expenditure including price, utilization and innovation. Although the increase in the price of medications mostly related to normal shifts in supply, a questionable business practices or market manipulation still have a role (Elisabeth Rosenthal 2014).

On the other hand, increase in number of users; length of hospitalization; dose of therapy; number of prescription; and the trend to replace the older and relatively less expensive medication by the newer and more expensive ones were the common contributors in pharmaceutical use and health-care delivery worldwide (Lublóy 2014; Aljunid 2007). However the biggest challenges over the next two decades were estimated to be the increase in life expectancy, changes in fertility and disease risk factors (Kaplan & Mathers 2011).

A significant number of cost analysis studies have been conducted covering different fields and establishing good ground in Southeast Asia (Aljunid et al. 2007; Tsilaajav 2005; Minh et al. 2009; Wang et al. 2014; Berman et al. 1989 & Riewpaiboon et al. 2005). The drug cost and the related factors have been discussed in many of local, regional and international studies, especially in hospital sector, covering various health economics fields. Unfortunately most of these studies tend to correlate the predicting factors with medical cost, drug cost, total hospital cost not the total pharmacy cost. Malaysian study conducted by Aljunid et al. (2007) focused on determining patient-related factors, treatment-related factors and provider-related factors influencing generic prescribing pattern and drug cost exclusively for cardiovascular patients in UKMMC. This study revealed that a significant relationship was observed between generic drug prescriptions with age of patients, types of wards and different levels of clinicians' training.

Tsilaajav (2005) recruited both of the step-down and bottom up costing methodologies to analyze data of 15 hospitals from the Philippine with emphasis on the top five common disease categories (Pneumonia, Acute bronchitis, Normal single delivery, Asthma, Senile cataract). This study found that with increasing the complexity and severity of conditions more and /or expensive drugs, diagnostic services and clinical expertise and sophisticated equipment are required. Also the unit cost results were significantly affected by the hospital length of stays.

Step down costing strategy on data collected from three rural district hospitals in Vietnam has been used by Minh et al. (2009) to estimate and analyze the "actual" unit cost of providing key clinical services. This study revealed that the user fee levels were much lower than the actual costs of providing the corresponding services.

The higher total hospital cost for management of lymphoma patients with chemotherapy-induced febrile neutropenia (FN) was associated the longer length of stay and severe sepsis among Singaporean patient as indicated by Wang et al. (2014). However, the main cost drivers were the medication costs and ward costs.

Indonesian costing study collected data from 173 facilities in 42 health centre work areas revealed that the drugs and supplies cost contributed to approximately of 43.3% of the total costs for curative care (Berman et al. 1989). Study done by Riewpaiboon et al. 2005 in Thailand aimed to explore cost structure of pharmacy department and propose more appropriate reimbursement method. This study revealed that the drug cost (acquisition cost) accounted for more than two third of the total pharmacy cost with the highest contribution 96% from the direct cost compared to 4% of the indirect cost.

2.13 CONCEPTUAL FRAMEWORK

Figure 2.1 describe the conceptual framework of this study. The aim of this study is to develop the MY-DRG casemix pharmacy inpatient service weights in UKM Medical Centre, Malaysia. The conceptual framework shows the costing methodology used to calculate the total pharmacy cost and to develop the casemix pharmacy inpatient service weights in UKM Medical Centre, in addition to the predicting factors of the total pharmacy cost.

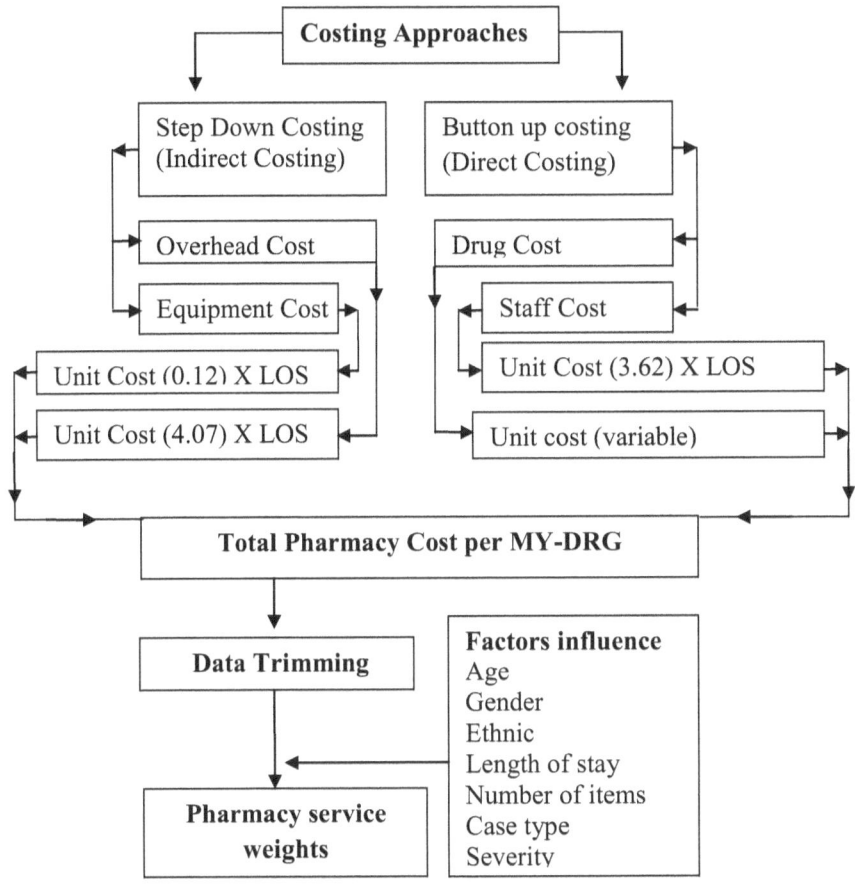

FIGURE 2.2 Flow Chart of Study

2.14 RESEARCH OBJECTIVES

2.14.1 General objective:

The main purpose of this study is to develop MY-DRG casemix pharmacy inpatient service weights in UKM Medical Centre, Malaysia

2.14.2 Specific objectives:

a. To conduct cost analysis of pharmacy patient services.
b. To calculate the total cost of pharmacy for inpatient cases.
c. To develop the casemix pharmacy service weights.
d. To determine the cost components of pharmacy services.
e. To predict factors that influence total cost of in-patient pharmacy services

2.15 HYPOTHESIS

a. Patients who have the longer length of stay in the hospital are more likely to have high total inpatient pharmacy cost.
b. Patients who have more items of prescribed drugs and supplies are more likely to have high the total inpatient pharmacy cost.
c. Patients who have undergone more complex procedures (surgical case) are more likely to have high the total inpatient pharmacy cost.
d. Patients who have higher level of severity are more likely to have high total inpatient pharmacy cost.
e. Patients in the older age groups are more likely to have high total inpatient pharmacy cost.
f. Male patients are more likely to have high total inpatient pharmacy cost than female patients.

2.16 CONCLUSION

A qualified and scientific Casemix team in UKM Medical Centre represented by International Casemix Centre and Clinical Coding (ITCC) unit in collaboration with United Nations University-International Institute For Global Health, has successfully developed Malaysian Diagnosis Related Group (MY-DRG). Three additional software were developed to facilitate the implementation of the Casemix system: the Data Tool Pro (coding software); the UNU-CBG Grouper; and Cost Modeling (CCM) software (costing software). Another important challenge in the way of implementing the casemix in UKM Medical Centre is to develop the MY-DRG service weights.

CHAPTER III
METHODOLOGY

3.1 INTRODUCTION

This chapter starts with short briefing about the study background and type of study design in addition to explanation of how to calculate the sample size and the relevant sampling methods. Study tool, data analysis, operational definition of variables and ethical consideration are presented in this chapter.

3.2 STUDY BACKGROUND

This is a retrospective study with data collected from inpatients pharmacy electronic prescription and the Casemix database of University Kebangsaan Malaysia Medical Center (UKMMC) of year 2011.

UKMMC provides a broad range of teaching and tertiary referral services in over 1,050 licensed inpatient beds, supported by extensive outpatient services, in addition to the primary emergency reception centre for the south eastern suburbs of Kuala Lumpur, the capital city of Malaysia.

In 2011, there were 384, 496 outpatients and 35, 303 inpatient episodes of services reported in this hospital (i.e. number of admissions or number of admitted patients). The total budget of the UKMMC was in excess of 473,523,579.09 million Malaysian Ringgit with a 3,453 total number of staff and covered area of 90,203.00 (m²).

UKMMC established the casemix unit in June 2002 and being the pioneer hospital that implemented Casemix system for inpatient management in Malaysia. The development of local cost weights was among many challenges that faced this program since its application. Our study will be the development of pharmacy services weight for MY-DRG for inpatient in UKMMC. We hope that this effort will be in the context of addressing these challenges.

3.3 STUDY DESIGN

A cross sectional design was employed to carry out a costing study in order to develop the casemix pharmacy services weights for inpatient cases of MY-DRG in UKM Medical Centre in 2011.

3.4 RESEARCH SETTING

This study was conducted in UKM Medical Centre in order to collect the intended data.

3.5 TARGET POPULATION

In this study, a costing strategy using mixed approach was employed by combining bottom-up and step-down costing methodologies to calculate the casemix pharmacy inpatient service weights in UKM Medical Centre. The required data (retrospective data) was the total of hospital expenditures for year 2011, total number of hospital staff, total floor area and total number of inpatients for the same year in UKM Medical Centre. While the data needed for bottom up costing approach were all the inpatient electronic-prescriptions and the total number of the inpatient pharmacy staff.

3.6 SAMPLING METHOD AND SAMPLE CALCULATION

The study used information on the pharmacy costs of all patients admitted to UKM Medical Centre from 1st January to 31st December 2011, comprising the 35, 303 discharges. The average length of stay (ALOS) of these patients was 5.5 days, representing 193,824 days of patient care.

Given the objective of ensuring highest rate of homogeneity for the combined data set, a number of exclusion criteria had to be specified which included the following:

a. Electronic-prescriptions with no date of prescription or has no corresponding MRN in the Casemix data were excluded.
b. Cases with no principle diagnosis were excluded.
c. Cases where the LOS value was not calculable due to errors in dates were excluded.
d. Cases where the age of patient was not calculable due to errors in dates were excluded.
e. Records where the gender and race were absent or not identifiable were excluded.
f. DRG where the severity of illness and case type was absent or not identifiable was excluded.

3.7 DATA ISSUES

The following steps have been done to develop the MY-DRG casemix pharmacy service weights in UKM Medical Centre by identifying the cost of pharmacy services by each MY-DRG casemix groups in the hospital.

3.7.1 Step One: Identifying the Pharmacy Component

In order to estimate the total costs of a particular health service, it is important to identify all the relevant costs and those who bear these costs. In this study the pharmacy component has been identified to include four main contributors:

a. The drugs and supplies cost.
b. The cost of in-patient pharmacy staff.
c. The pharmacy use of the overhead cost centers allocation.
d. The pharmacy equipment cost.

3.7.2 Step Two: Source of Data and DRG Assignment

Data on this study has been collected from three main sources:

a. Information on the drugs /medicines, fluids and medical supplies prescribed to the patient was obtained from electronic-prescription system on Excel based file. Electronic prescribing refers to the ordering, administration and supply of drugs which is completely supported by electronic systems. Each e-prescription defined as one episode (a period of inpatient care) having data on medical registration number (MRN) which is a unique number given for each local and international client; name of the patient; e-prescription number; date of prescription; number of items, quantity, duration and the name of the prescribed medicines, fluids and supplies.
b. The casemix database of UKM Medical Centre of year 2011 obtained from the health information department having data on MRN, ethnicity, ward, date of admission, date of discharge, birth day (age at admission), gender, length of stay, primary and secondary diagnosis up 30 diagnosis, MY-DRGs, case type (medical and surgical) and the level of severity of illness.
c. Costing template from the financial department having data on UKM Medical Centre including the total number of staff, pharmacy staff, and the floor area, total annual allocation of each of the overhead cost centers, equipment cost and the total purchase of the last five years.

These data have been joined manually using the medical registration number and data of admission to produce one set of data for analysis.

Finally for each patient (episode) we have the patient's name, ethnicity, MRN, date of admission, date of discharge, birth day (age at admission), length of stay, gender, MY-DRG, case type (medical or surgical), level of the severity of illness, description of cases, number of items and quantity of drugs and supplies prescribed per patient/episode, and the unit price of each item.

3.7.3 Step Three: Calculation of the Total Pharmacy Cost

A mixed approach which is based partly on step-down (top-down) and partly on bottom up or activity based (ABC) costing methodology has been recruited in order to calculate the pharmacy cost per patient or episodes. The required data (retrospective data) for ABC approach were the all inpatient e-prescriptions and the total number of the inpatient pharmacy staff for year 2011 in UKM Medical Centre. While the data needed for top down costing were the total of hospital expenditures, total number of hospital staff, total hospital floor area and total number of inpatients for year 2011, in UKM Medical Centre.

   a. Step-down costing:

   The main purpose of this step is to determine the pharmacy use of the indirect (overhead) cost centers. Normally starts (at the top) with total expenditures and then divides these by a measure of total output (e.g. patient visits, days or admissions) to give an "average" cost per patient per visit, per day or per admission.

   i. The pharmacy use of the overhead cost centers and allocation factors

   Data on the annual total cost for each overhead cost center has been collected from the financial department of UKM Medical Centre. An appropriate allocation factors used to determine the pharmacy use of the indirect (overhead) cost centers. One the following questions have been used to calculate the pharmacy use of each of the overhead cost centers:

The pharmacy use of the indirect (overhead) cost centers = (Number of pharmacy staff / total number of hospital staff) x (annual total overhead cost centre).

Or

The pharmacy use of the indirect (overhead) cost centers = (pharmacy floor area / total hospital floor area) x (annual total overhead cost centre).

Summing up all the allocations gave the total pharmacy use of the indirect (overhead) cost centers. Then the total pharmacy use of the indirect (overhead) cost centers multiplied by the proportion of inpatient pharmacy services to get the inpatient pharmacy use of the indirect (overhead) cost centers.

The results of this question divided by total annual number of (inpatient days) to get the inpatient pharmacy use cost per day. This unit cost in the question was then multiplied by (the length of stay) of investigated patient to get the inpatient pharmacy use cost per patient per day.

ii. The pharmacy equipment cost (capital costs)

Data on the total UKM Medical Centre pharmacy department capital costs was obtained from the financial department in the hospital. All the purchased or donated equipments, furniture and vehicles in the last 5 years were included. The total capital cost has been divided by Annualization Factor at 5% discount rate. The result has been multiplied by inpatient proportion which already determined by The UKM Medical Centre pharmacy office. Then the inpatient pharmacy capital asset costs divided by the total number of (inpatient days) to get the capital assets cost per day. This unit cost in the question was multiplied by length of stay of each investigated patient to get the inpatient pharmacy capital assets cost per patient per day.

b. Bottom-up or Activity based costing and data collection

   The Bottom-up costing requires recording of every item of service that a patient receives, and changing them into costs. Bottom-up costing gives more accurate results, but it requires a large investment in time and resources. In this study, the bottom-up approach was used to estimate drug and supply cost per episode; and to cost inpatient staff of the pharmacy per patient.

   i. Costs of pharmacy staff serviced inpatients

      Direct cost for staff cost covered all in-patient pharmacy staff responsible for supplying medications to all wards and units in UKM Medical Centre. Basic salaries and additional allowances, bonuses, contributions, payments were obtained from the staff directly and confirmed by hospital personnel services administrative records. Summing up all in-patient pharmacy staff costs gave the total staff cost. Then the total staff cost was divided by total annual number of (inpatient days) to get staff cost per day. This unit cost was then multiplied by (length of stay) of investigated patient to estimate staff cost per patient per day.

   ii. Cost of inpatient drugs/medicines and medical supplies

      All the drugs/medicines, fluids and medical supplies prescribed to the patient in one complete episode of care have been included. Drugs prescribed and purchased by patients to take home were excluded. List of acquisition unit costs (price) of each drug and supplies were obtained from the UKM Medical Centre pharmacy office. This unit cost was then multiplied by the quantity of the corresponding item to estimate cost per item. Then we summed up the cost of all items in one e-prescription to estimate drug cost per patient (per episode).

3.7.3 Calculation of patient level total pharmacy costs

The total pharmacy cost of each individual patient /episode would be the summing of total drugs and supplies cost plus the results of multiplying the estimated unit cost of each of (pharmacy use of overhead cost centers; the pharmacy equipment cost; pharmacy staff cost) by the LOS of investigated patient/episode.

3.7.4 Step Four: Data Trimming

The L3H3 method (L three H three), is data trimming method commonly used to ensure that the means reported more accurately represent the central tendency amongst cases analyzed. This method mainly consists of using the average pharmacy cost for every MY-DRG having more than 20 patient/episode divided by three as the low trim point and the average pharmacy cost multiplied by three as the high trim point. So, in term of distribution the normal cases in each MY-DRG lie inside the two trim points: (the lowest point is one third of the average pharmacy cost and the highest point is three times of the average pharmacy cost) and known as inliers. In contrast, the cases which lie outside the trim points considered skewed or outlier cases and have been excluded from analysis.

3.7.5 Step Five: Calculation the Pharmacy Service Weight per each MY-DRG

Pharmacy service weight was defined as the burden of work or services performed by pharmacy component and the resources used for a patient compared to the burden of other services for others DRGs. The actual service weights are unit less numbers that express the expected cost for one visit in relation to average visit. The best way to calculate service weights is to use actual cost per inpatient case by assigning each DRG a relative value that reflects the cost of any one, or all, of the resources consumed (e.g. bed-days, theatre time, drugs, diagnostic procedures, physiotherapy and nursing treatment) in that respective DRG when compared with all DRGs.

In order to estimate the pharmacy service weight we need first to calculate the average pharmacy cost for all MY-DRGs. The closest average cost among all the MY-DRGs would be the base used to calculate the pharmacy service weight using the following question:

Pharmacy service weight of a MY-DRG = Average pharmacy cost of the investigated MY-DRG / Average of a specified MY-DRG (which usually the average pharmacy cost of all MY-DRGs).

3.8 INCLUSION AND EXCLUSION CRITERIA

3.8.1 Inclusion criteria for patients

a. All inpatients admitted in year 2011 in UKM Medical Centre.
b. All inpatients in the electronic-prescription record in year 2011 in UKM Medical Centre.

3.8.2 Exclusion criteria for patients

a. Patients attending outpatients, emergency department, and UKM specialist centre.
b. All inpatients admitted in other years than 2011 UKM Medical Centre.

c. All inpatients admitted in 2011 in UKM Medical Centre but without complete data in Casemix Database and e-prescription database.

3.10 ETHICS

This study was approved by ethics committee of National University of Malaysia- Medical Center (UKMMC), code number (UNU-002-2013) in 20 May 2013.

3.11 VARIABLES

3.11.1 Dependent Variables

- The total inpatient Pharmacy cost.

3.11.2 Independent Variables

a. Age.
b. Gender.
c. Ethnicity.
d. Length of stay.
e. Number of items of drugs and supplies prescribed in e-prescription.
f. Type of cases (medical or surgical).
g. Level of severity of illness (level I, level II, level III).

3.12 DATA ANALYSIS

All available data was gathered and entered into the database. The main analysis process includes mixed costing approach (step-down and activity base costing). Statistical Software, "Statistical package for social science version 16" (SPSS) has been used to answer the study objectives.

Step-down approach used to analyze data related to pharmacy use of the overhead cost centres allocation and the pharmacy equipment cost (indirect cost), while the activity based costing approach was used to analyze data related to drugs and supplies cost and inpatient pharmacy staff cost. The clinical and demographic characteristics were reported for each patient based on episode of care (admission and discharge). Descriptive analyses, exploratory analyses, bivariate analyses and multiple linear regression analyses were conducted to predict the total inpatient pharmacy cost from various potential predictors.

3.13 OPERATIONAL DEFINITION

a. Pharmacy cost: Defined as the capital and recurrent cost of all drugs and supplies prescribed to patients during their admission episodes in UKM Medical Centre in 2011.
b. Age of patient: Defined as the age of patient based on the last birthday on the day the patient is admitted to UK Medical Centre.
c. Gender: The category to which an individual is assigned on the basis of sex (category: male = 1, female = 2).
d. Length of stay (LOS): The duration of patient stay in the ward from admission until his/her discharge. LOS was measured for each episode /patient by applying the following equation: (date of discharge - date of admission) + one.
e. Number of items of drugs and supplies: Defined as the number of drugs and supplies prescribed in each e-prescription within each episode of in-patient stay.
f. Cases types: Patients are categorized into two case types i.e. Medical and Surgical Case. Medical cases are patients who were admitted to medical-based discipline ward without any major procedures. Surgical cases are patients who were admitted to surgical-based discipline wards and usually undergone major surgical procedures.

g. Severity of cases: Severity of patient's illness was coded 1, 2 or 3 (with increasing severity), based on presence of co-morbidity, complications, age and discharge status. The assignment is based on the logic of MY-DRG Grouper. Under the MY-DRG, severity level 1, when the patients did not suffer from any complication or pre-existing co morbidity. Severity level 2 implicates that the patient suffers from minor complications (with a second diagnosis) and co morbidity that prolongs the length of patients' stay by one day. While severity level 3 when the patient had a major complication and co morbidity that prolonged the in-patient stay.

h. Capital cost: defined as the cost of items with more than one year life-span but with the unit cost of (RM1000 and above). This includes, building, equipment etc.).

i. Recurrent cost: defined as the cost of any items with life-span of less than one year including capital items with unit cost value of below (RM1000).

j. Overhead Cost Centers: Cost centres providing general services which are not directly related to patient care. The cost of these health centres are shared with all units or departments in UKMMC. These cost centres allocate but do not receive cost from other cost centres. These cost centers include, among other administration office, maintenance, library, IT centre, general store and consumables, utility (water and electricity), telephone and fax service, cleaning services, security, taxes and insurance, rental and CSSD services.

k. Intermediate cost centres: These cost centres, receive resources from overhead cost centres and provide the support services to final cost centres. These cost centres, among others are laboratory, radiology, pharmacy, physiotherapy, operation theatre and intensive care unit, occupational therapy, Coronary Care unit (CCU), Coronary Rehabilitation ward (CRW), Neonatal Intensive care unit, Pediatric ICU.

l. Final cost centers: These cost-centres receive cost from overhead and intermediate cost centres and provide services directly to patients. In this study, the inpatient cost centres include medical ward, surgical ward, pediatric ward and O&G ward.
m. Pharmacy services: is defined as "an action or set of actions undertaken in or organized by a pharmacy, delivered by a pharmacist or other health practitioner, who applies their specialized health knowledge personally or via an intermediary, with a patient/client, population or other health professional, to optimize the process of care, with the aim to improve health outcomes and the value of healthcare."
n. Pharmacy service weight: The burden of work or services performed by pharmacy component and the resources used for a patient compared to the burden of other services for others DRGs.

3.14 CONCLUSION

A lot of expenses, efforts and time were saved by availability of two sets of data namely: e-prescription data and casemix database. Furthermore it facilitated the conduction of this costing study by applying the step-down and bottom-up costing methodologies to estimate the total inpatient pharmacy cost and developing the casemix pharmacy in-patient cost weights in UKM Medical Centre.

CHAPTER IV
RESULTS

4.1 INTRODUCTION

This chapter presents the results of the study. The results are presented in three (3) major sections. First section discusses the descriptive and analysis of the steps used to calculate the total pharmacy cost (n=20,192). In the second section we presented the descriptive, bivariate and multivariate regression analysis of the trimmed data (n=13,673) used to predict factors influencing the study outcome (the total inpatient pharmacy cost). In the third section, development of the MY-DRG casemix pharmacy service weights is discussed.

4.2 DESCRIPTIVE RESULTS

4.2.1 Patient Level Data

The UKM Medical Centre total inpatient admissions in 2011 was 35, 303, of which 31.270 (88.58%) inpatient cases have an electronic prescription records. Then out of these 31.270 inpatient cases that have an e-prescription records, 20,192 (64.57%) were found to have corresponding casemix inpatients codes.

4.2.2 Socio Demographic and Clinical Background of Patients

Table 4.1 and table 4 2. Present the socio demographic and clinical background of the 20,192 patients. The average age of patients was 43.69 years (SD 23.28) (0-107) of which 8, 988 (44.5%) were males and 11,204 (55.5%) were females. Majority of patients were Malay (46.9%), followed by Chinese (27.0%), Indian (15.4%) and others (10.7%) respectively.

Majority of patients were diagnosed as a medical cases (69.2%) compared to (30.8%) diagnosed as a surgical cases. 49.4% (n=9,984) patients were of severity level 1, 33.4% (n=6,744) patients were of severity level 2 and 17.2% (n=3,464 patients) were from severity level 3 respectively.

The range of length of stay varied from 1 to 69 days with average length of stay is 6.58 (SD 7.58) days and median of 4 days. About 64.3% (n=12,987) were patients with length of stay of less than six days and the highest proportion of patients (16.4%), (20.6%) and (13.9%) were separated on the second and third and fourth days after admission respectively.

The total number of drugs and supplies (items) prescribed for all 20,192 patients were 216,613 items (drugs and supplies) with average of 10.73 (SD12.59) and median of 7 items.

About 61.9% were patients with number of prescription of less than ten. The highest number of drugs and supplies (items) prescribed to patient admitted under the MY-DRG code of V-1-12-I (Complex Prostate & Scrotal Operation with Minor Complications and Co-morbidity).

The total pharmacy cost calculated for all 20,192 patients was RM 7,400,998.05. The mean cost for each patient is RM366.53 (SD RM1, 126.70) with median cost of RM90.10 and Inerquartile range of 207.15.

Table 4.1 Descriptive statistics of age, length of stay, number of items and total pharmacy cost of patients (n=20,192)

Factors	Mean	Median	SD	Min.	Max.
Age	43.69	44.00	23.28	0.0	107
Number of items	10.73	7.00	12.59	1	201
Length of stay	6.58	4.00	7.58	1	69
Total pharmacy cost	366.53	90.10	1,126.70	7.84	44,548.28

Table 4.2 Socio demographic and clinical characteristics of categorical variables of patients (n= 20, 192)

Characteristics	Category	N	%
Age group	0-19 Years old	3,021	15.0
	20-39 Years old	6,417	31.8
	40-59 Years old	4,343	21.5
	= or > 60 Years old	6,411	31.8
Gender	Male	8,988	44.5
	Female	11,204	55.5
Case type	Medical	13,974	69.2
	Surgical	6,218	30.8
Severity of illness	Severity level I	9,984	49.4
	Severity level II	6,744	33.4
	Severity level III	3,464	17.2
Ethnicity	Malay	9,475	46.9
	Chinese	5,455	27.0
	Indian	3,100	15.4
	Others	2,162	10.7

4.2.3 DRG Assignment

In this study, over 20,192 inpatient electronic-prescriptions with ALOS of 6.6 days were assigned to 633 DRGs. DRG O-6-12-I, Vaginal Delivery with other Procedure Excluding Sterilization &/Or Dilation & Curettage (3.75%), was the highest volume DRG identified in this study with 758 cases.

4.2.4 Casemix Major Groups Assignment

Out of 32 Casemix Major Groups (CMG) codes and description used in MY-DRG, 22 (68.75%) categories have been used. The highest volume 2,655 (13.15%) was the Deliveries Groups (O). The lowest volume 15 (0.07%) was the Newborn and Neonates Groups (P). Table 4.3 presents the number and percent of cases in each of the 22 CMG used by this study. Five of CMG namely: Deliveries Groups (O), Digestive system Groups (K), cardiovascular system Groups (I), musculoskeletal system & connective tissue Groups (M), Respiratory system Groups (J) contributed to approximately 10,129 (50.36%) of total CMG assignment, table 4.3.

Table 4.3 Casemix Major Groups (CMG) codes used in MY-DRG (n= 20,192)

No.	CMG Codes	Description	N	%
1	A	Infectious & parasitic diseases Groups	546	2.70
2	B	Hepatobiliary & pancreatic system Groups	650	3.22
3	C	Myeloproliferative system & neoplasms Groups	443	2.19
4	D	Haemopoeitic & immune system Groups	299	1.48

5	E	Endocrine system, nutrition & metabolism Groups	531	2.63
6	F	Mental Health and Behavioral Groups	425	2.10
7	G	Central nervous system Groups	1,307	6.47
8	H	Eye and Adnexa Groups	570	2.82
9	I	Cardiovascular system Groups	1,969	9.75
10	J	Respiratory system Groups	1,698	8.41
11	K	Digestive system Groups	1,985	9.83
12	L	Skin, subcutaneous tissue & breast Groups	978	4.84
13	M	Musculoskeletal system & connective tissue Groups	1,822	9.02
14	N	Nephro-urinary System Groups	1,215	6.02
15	O	Deliveries Groups	2,655	13.15
16	P	Newborns & Neonates Groups	15	0.07
17	S	Injuries, poisonings & toxic effects of drugs Groups	163	0.81
18	T	Substance abuse & dependence Groups	16	0.08
19	U	Ear, nose, mouth & throat Groups	899	4.45
20	V	Male reproductive System Groups	302	1.50
21	W	Female reproductive system Groups	1,613	7.99
22	Z	Factors influencing health status & other contacts with health services Groups	91	0.45
		Total	20,192	100.00

4.3 CALCULATION OF THE TOTAL PHARMACY COST

In order to calculate the total pharmacy cost for each MY-DRG, the unit costs of each of the four components of the pharmacy (drugs and supplies cost, cost of inpatient pharmacy staff, pharmacy use of the overhead cost centers allocation and the pharmacy equipment cost) was estimated as follows:

4.3.1 Unit Cost of the Pharmacy Use of the Overhead Cost Centers Allocation

The total pharmacy use of the overhead cost centers was calculated from twelve cost centers namely: the administration, maintenance, utility, cleaning services, security, general store and consumable, information technology (IT) centre, library, tax and insurance, rent, the central sterile services department (CSSD), telephone and fax centers.

Table 4.4 shows the overhead cost centers and the appropriate allocation factors used to determine the pharmacy use of the indirect (overhead) cost centers. Allocation factors are only based on two crude criteria, 3.56% for proportion of number of staff and 2.42% for the proportion of the floor area. The highest allocation MR 1,866,136.77 (37.82%) was from the administration centers [(total pharmacy staff is 123 / total UKMMC staff 3, 453) X total Annual administration staff cost 52, 388,376.06]. Three centers, namely: administration, maintenance and general store and consumable contributed to about three quarter (72.79%) of all the overhead cost centres allocation. The lowest allocation was 6,779.85 (0.14%) was from the security centre [(Pharmacy floor area is 2,187 m^2 / total UKMMC floor area 90, 230.0 m^2) X total annual security staff cost 297, 719.32]. Figure 2 shows the percentage of the pharmacy use from these twelve over head cost centers. The total pharmacy use of the indirect (overhead) cost centers (RM 4,934,094.08) was multiplied by the inpatient proportion (16%) to get the inpatient pharmacy use of the indirect (overhead) cost centers (RM789,455.05).

The inpatient pharmacy use cost per day was obtained by dividing the inpatient pharmacy use of the indirect (overhead) cost centers allocation (RM789, 455.05) by the total annual number of UKMMC inpatient days (193,824). Finally this unit cost (4.07) was then multiplied by (the length of stays) of each investigated patient to get the inpatient pharmacy use cost per patient per day.

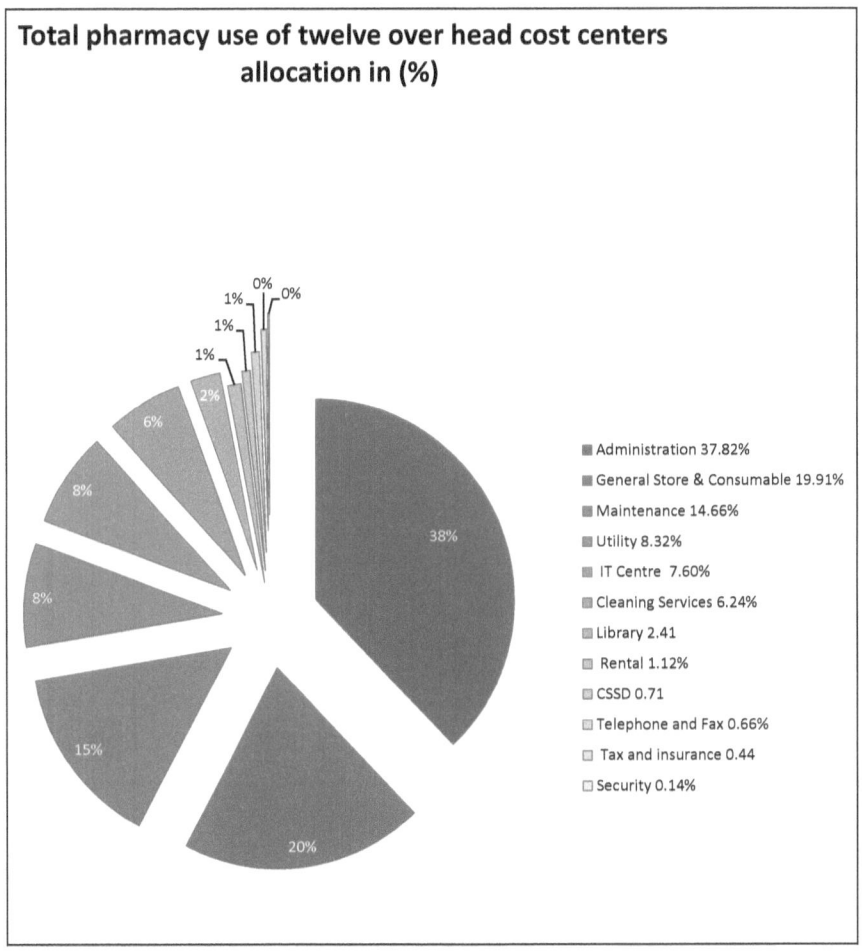

FIGURE 4.1 Total pharmacy uses of twelve overhead cost centres allocation in (%).

Source: Study Results

Table 4.4 Pharmacy use of the overhead cost centers and the allocation factors

Overhead cost centre	Allocation Factor		Annual staff cost (RM)	Total pharmacy use of overhead allocation (RM)	
	Number of staff	Floor Area (m^2)			
Administration	NS*	-	52,388,376.06	1,866,136.77	37.82
Maintenance	-	FA**	29,842,623.45	723,327.25	14.66
Utility	-	FA	16,929,629.03	410,341.34	8.32
Cleaning Services	-	FA	12,697,344.58	307,758.98	6.24
Security	-	FA	279,719.32	6,779.85	0.14
General Store & Consumable	NS	-	27,571,810.25	982,140.94	19.91
IT Centre	NS	-	10,522,783.52	374,834.17	7.60
Library	NS	-	3,332,106.52	118,693.63	2.41
Tax and insurance	NS	-	603,542.24	21,498.90	0.44
Rental	NS	-	1,545,306.84	55,045.68	1.12
CSSD	-	FA	1,441,210.82	34,932.15	0.71
Telephone and Fax	NS	-	915,309.98	32,604.44	0.66
Total			158,069,762.61	4,934,094.08	100.00
Pharmacy	123	2,187			
UKMMC	3,453	90,230.00			

*NS (number of staff), **FA (floor area)

4.3.2 Unit Cost of the Pharmacy Equipment Cost (Capital Costs)

The total pharmacy capital costs were calculated by summing up the costs of all the purchased or donated equipments, furniture and vehicles in the last 5 years (RM 642,375.16). The pharmacy building cost was excluded.

The total capital cost was divided by Annualization Factor (4.32) at 5% discount rate. The result (RM148, 697.95) was multiplied by inpatient proportion (16%). Then the inpatient pharmacy capital asset costs (RM 23, 791.67) divided by the total number of inpatient days (193,824) to get the capital assets cost per day.

Finally this unit cost (0.12) in the question was multiplied by length of stays of each investigated patient to get the inpatient pharmacy capital assets cost per patient per day.

4.3.3 Unit Cost of the Pharmacy Staff Serviced Inpatients

Out of 123 total UKMMC pharmacy staff, 20 (16%) were the pharmacy staff those serviced inpatients wards. The total inpatient pharmacy staff cost (RM 702,030.48) was obtained by summing up the basic salaries and additional allowances, bonuses, contributions, payments to the inpatient pharmacy staff, table 4.5.

Then the total staff cost was divided by total annual number of inpatient days (193,824) to get staff cost per day. Finally this unit cost (3.62) was then multiplied by (length of stay) of each investigated patient to estimate staff cost per patient per day.

4.3.4 Unit Cost of inpatient drugs/medicines and medical supplies

The total drug and supplies cost was calculated for each investigated patient (episode) separately by multiplying the unit cost (price) of each drug and supplies by the quantity of the corresponding item to estimate cost per item. Then we summed up the cost of all items in one e-prescription to estimate drug cost per patient (per episode).

Table 4.5   UKMMC inpatient pharmacy staff salary, 2011 (n=20)

No.	Grade	Service By Year	Salary (RM)	Annual Salary (RM)
1	U54	17	9,221.12	110,653.44
2	U54	15	8,761.92	105,143.04
3	U54	13	8,302.72	99,632.64
4	U48	7	5,945.48	71,345.76
5	U32	15	3,323.58	39,882.96
6	U32	20	3,845.41	46,144.92
7	U29	11	1,938.62	23,263.44
8	U29	9	1,797.45	21,569.4
9	U29	3	1,303.37	15,640.44
10	U29	8	1,726.87	20,722.44
11	U29	7	1,656.29	19,875.48
12	U29	4	1,444.54	17,334.48
13	U12	16	1,523.89	18,286.68
14	U3	5	922.48	11,069.76
15	U3	10	1,141.37	13,696.44
16	U3	2	795.07	9,540.84
17	U3	15	1,379.86	16,558.32
18	U3	2	795.07	9,540.84
19	U3	1	752.6	9,031.2
20	N17	6	1,924.83	23,097.96
		Total	58,502.54	702,030.48

Source: UKMMC pharmacy office

4.3.5 Calculation of Patient Level Total Pharmacy Costs

The total pharmacy cost was calculated for each individual patient (episode) by summing up (the total drugs and supplies cost, the inpatient pharmacy use of overhead cost centers, the pharmacy equipment cost and the pharmacy staff cost) then multiplied by the LOS of each investigated patient/episode. In this study, over 20,192 patients have been included which was huge data and impossible to be presented in one table. For the purpose of explanation we produced one table as sample and the rest of data has been kept in software results and available upon request from UKMMC.

Table 4.6 shows the estimated unit costs of the pharmacy components with exception of the drugs and supplies unit cost which is variable depending on the number of items and the quantity of drugs and supplies consumed by each patient (episode).

Table 4.6 Sample of the total pharmacy cost calculation per patient/episode (n = 15 out of 20,192)

NO.	MRN	MY-DRG	LOS	Direct cost		Indirect cost			Total pharmacy Cost Per patient (episode)
				Drug & supplies Unit cost variable	Pharmacy staff Unit cost 3.62	Overhead Cost Unit cost 4.07	Equipment Unit cost 0.12		
1	M628631	A-4-10-I	18.00	55.95	65.16	73.26	2.16		196.53
2	M772213	A-4-10-I	8.00	1,133.86	28.96	32.56	0.96		1,196.34
3	N352247	A-4-10-I	4.00	3.91	14.48	16.28	0.48		35.15
4	M248583	A-4-10-II	66.00	3,386.11	238.92	268.62	7.92		3,901.57
5	N330792	A-4-10-II	31.00	8,271.16	112.22	126.17	3.72		8,513.27
6	N331313	A-4-10-II	31.00	1,485.85	112.22	126.17	3.72		1,727.96
7	N134994	A-4-10-II	31.00	1,448.73	112.22	126.17	3.72		1,690.84
8	N332480	A-4-10-II	28.00	3,448.17	101.36	113.96	3.36		3,666.85
9	N344550	A-4-10-II	27.00	1,465.96	97.74	109.89	3.24		1,676.83
10	M948613	A-4-10-II	26.00	660.27	94.12	105.82	3.12		863.33
11	M169671	A-4-10-II	24.00	4,954.08	86.88	97.68	2.88		5,141.52
12	M169345	A-4-10-II	24.00	1,788.67	86.88	97.68	2.88		1,976.11
13	M454191	A-4-10-II	20.00	406.28	72.4	81.4	2.4		562.48
14	N268917	A-4-10-II	19.00	747.99	68.78	77.33	2.28		896.38
15	M239618	A-4-10-II	18.00	856.33	65.16	73.26	2.16		996.91

4.3.6 Total Pharmacy Cost

The total pharmacy cost of 20,192 patients was (RM 7,400,412.26) with average of (RM 366.53 per patient). Drugs and supplies were the main component (86.0%) of pharmacy cost compared to pharmacy use of the overhead cost centers allocation (7.30%), inpatient pharmacy staff cost (6.50%) and inpatient pharmacy equipments (0.20%) respectively. Table 4.7 presents the total and the average of inpatient pharmacy components cost.

Table 4.7   Inpatient pharmacy cost components (n=20,192)

No.	Pharmacy Components	Total (RM)	Average	%
1	Total drugs and supplies cost	6,363,283.31	315.15	86.00
2	Pharmacy staff cost	480,717.9	23.81	6.50
3	Pharmacy use of overhead cost centers	540,475.65	26.78	7.30
4	Pharmacy equipment cost	15,935.4	0.79	0.20
	Total pharmacy cost (n=20,192)	7,400,412.26	366.53	100.00

4.4 PREDICTING FACTORS INFLUENCING THE STUDY OUTCOME

A set of combination of socio demographic and clinical factors was recruited to predict the study outcome (the total inpatient pharmacy cost). This study used the L3H3 (L three H three) data trimming method to ensure that the means (the average pharmacy cost for every MY-DRG) reported more accurately represent the central tendency amongst cases analyzed and to exclude the outliers from analysis. Out of 20,192 patients, only 13, 673 (67.71%) patients/episodes were available for final analyses after the data trimming.

4.5 DESCRIPTIVE ANALYSES

Table 4.8 and table 4.9 present the socio demographic and clinical background of the 13, 673 patients from trimmed database. The average age of respondents was 43.53 years (SD 22.28) (0-107) of which 5,767 (42.2%) were males and 7,906 (57.8%) were females.

Majority of patients were Malay (49.3%), followed by Chinese (27.8%), Indian (13.8%), others (9.1%) respectively. Majority of patients were diagnosed as a medical cases (61.9%) compared to (38.1%) diagnosed as a surgical cases. 53.6% (n=7,329) patients were of severity level I, 30.8% (n=4,210) patients were of severity level II and 15.6% (n=2,134 patients) were from severity level III respectively.

The range of length of stay varied from 1 to 69 days with average length of stay is 6.76 (SD 7.16) days and median of 4 days. About 61.2% (n=8,378) were patients with length of stay of less than six days and the highest proportion of patients (13.5%), (19.9%) and (15.2%) separated on the second, third and fourth days after admission respectively.

The total number of drugs and supplies (items) prescribed for all 13,673 patients were over 111,794 items with average of 8.18 (SD5.81) and median of 6 items.

About 68.0% were patients with number of prescription of less than ten items. The total pharmacy cost calculated for all 13,673 patients was (RM 4,326,458.36). The mean cost for each patient is RM316.42 (SD RM176.75) with median cost of RM109.65.

Table 4.8   Descriptive statistics of age, length of stay, number of items and total pharmacy cost of patients (Trimmed data, n=13,673)

Characteristics	Mean	Median	S.D.	Min.	Max.
Age (Years)	43.53	40.00	22.28	0.0	107
Number of items (Pharmacy)	8.18	6.00	5.81	1	25
Length of stay (Days)	6.76	4.00	7.16	1	69
Total pharmacy cost (RM)	316.42	109.95	176.75	7.84	19,890.33

Table 4.9 Socio demographic and clinical characteristics of categorical variables of patients (Trimmed data, n=13,673)

Characteristics	Category	N	%
Age group	0-19 Years old	1,678	12.3
	20-39 Years old	5,058	37.0
	40-59 Years old	2,820	20.6
	= or > 60 Years old	4,117	30.1
Gender	Male	5,767	42.2
	Female	7,906	57.8
Case type	Medical	8,469	61.9
	Surgical	5,204	38.1
Severity of illness	Severity level I	7,329	53.6
	Severity level II	4,210	30.8
	Severity level III	2,134	15.6
Ethnicity	Malay	6,738	49.3
	Chinese	3,801	27.8
	Indian	1,887	13.8
	Others	1,247	9.1

4.6 STUDY OF OUTLIERS

All cases which lay outside the trim points considered skewed or outlier cases and have been excluded from analysis. Over 6,519 (32.29%) patients were found as outlier and have been excluded from analyses.

4.6.1 Descriptive Analysis

Table 4.10 and table 4.11 present the socio demographic and clinical background of the 6,519 outlier's patients. The average age of outlier's patient was 44.05 years (SD 25.25) (0-104) of which 3,221 (49.4%) were males and 3,298 (50.6%) were females. Majority of patients were Malay (42.0%), followed by Chinese (25.4%), Indian (18.6%), others (14.0%) respectively. Majority of patients were diagnosed as a medical cases (84.4%) compared to (15.6%) diagnosed as a surgical cases. 40.7% (n=2,655) patients were of severity level I, 38.9% (n=2,534) patients were of severity level II and 20.4% (n=1,330 patients) were from severity level III respectively.

The range of length of stay varied from 1 to 69 days with average length of stay is 6.20 (SD 8.38) days and median of 3 days. About 70.7% (n=4,608) were patients with length of stay of less than six days and the highest proportion of patients (22.4%), (22.0%) and (11.2%) separated on the second, third and fourth days after admission respectively.

The total number of drugs and supplies (items) prescribed for all 6,519 outlier patients were over 104,819 items with average of 17.37 (SD19.01) and median of 11items.

About 45.3% were patients with number of prescription of less than ten items. The total pharmacy cost calculated for all 6,519 patients was (RM 3,074,539.69). The mean cost for each patient is RM471.63 (SD RM1, 642.85) with median cost of RM50.53.

Table 4.10 Descriptive statistics of age, length of stay, number of items and total pharmacy cost of patients (Outliers, n= 6,519)

Factors	Mean	Median	S.D.	Min.	Max.
Age (Years)	44.05	49.00	25.25	0.0	104
Number of items (Pharmacy)	17.37	11.00	19.01	1	201
Length of stay (Days)	6.20	3.00	8.38	1	69
Total pharmacy cost (RM)	471.63	50.53	1,642.85	7.84	4,548.28

Table 4.11 Socio demographic and clinical characteristics of categorical variables of patients (Outliers, n= 6,519)

Factors	Category	N	%
Age group	0-19 Years old	1,342	20.6
	20-39 Years old	1,359	20.8
	40-59 Years old	1,524	23.4
	= or > 60 Years old	2,294	35.2
Gender	Male	3,221	49.4
	Female	3,298	50.6
Case type	Medical	5,505	84.4
	Surgical	1,014	15.6
Severity of illness	Severity level I	2,655	40.7
	Severity level II	2,534	38.9
	Severity level III	1,330	20.4
Ethnicity	Malay	2,737	42.0
	Chinese	1,654	25.4
	Indian	1,213	18.6
	Others	915	14.0

4.7 BIVARIATE ANALYSIS TO PREDICT TOTAL PHARMACY COST

Based on Kolmogorov-Simrnov test, the data was normally distributed, therefore the statistical analysis which used in this study was parametric test such as, Pearson correlation and one way ANOVA test.

4.7.1 Association Between Age of Patients and Total Pharmacy Cost

A Pearson product-moment correlation was run to determine the relationship between age of patients (in years) and the total inpatient pharmacy cost. There was fair, positive correlation between age and the total pharmacy cost, which was statistically significant ($r = 0.147$, $n = 13673$, $p < 0.0001$).

4.7.2 Association Between Length of Stay and Total Pharmacy Cost

A Pearson product-moment correlation was run to determine the relationship between length of stay (in days) and the total inpatient pharmacy cost. There was strong, positive correlation length of stay and the total inpatient pharmacy cost, which was statistically significant ($r = 0.502$, $n = 13,673$, $p < 0.0001$).

4.7.3 Association Between Number of Items and Total Pharmacy Cost

A Pearson product-moment correlation was run to determine the relationship between number of items and the total inpatient pharmacy cost. There was strong, positive correlation number of items and the total inpatient pharmacy cost, which was statistically significant ($r = 0.376$, $n = 13,673$, $p < 0.0001$), table 4.12.

Table 4.12 Correlation between age, length of stay, number of items and total inpatient pharmacy cost (Trimmed data, n=13,673)

Factors	Total pharmacy cost	
	r	Sig.
Age	0.147	0.000
Length of stay	0.502	0.000
No. of items	0.376	0.000

4.7.4 Association between Gender and Total Pharmacy Cost

An independent –sample t-test was run to determine if there were differences in total pharmacy cost between males and females. Total inpatient pharmacy cost was more among males (m= 397.11, SD=84.50) than females (m= 257.56, SD=68.89), a statistically significant difference, m=139.55, 95%CI [112.97, 166.13], t (10851.317) =10.292, $P=$ <0.001.

4.7.5 Association between Type of Cases and Total Pharmacy Cost

An independent –sample t-test was run to determine if there were differences in total pharmacy cost between medical and surgical cases. Total inpatient pharmacy cost was more among surgical cases (m= 349.89, SD=72.89) than medical cases (m= 261.96, SD=80.95), a statistically significant difference, m=87.93, 95%CI [61.00, 114.85], t (10132.631) =6.402, $P=$ <0.001.

4.7.6 Association between Ethnicity and Total Pharmacy Cost

A one-way between-groups analysis of variance was conducted to explore the impact of ethnicity on the total pharmacy cost. Ethnicity was divided into four groups (group 1: Malay; group 2: Chinese; group 3: Indian; group 4: others).

There was a statistically significant difference between groups as determined by one-way ANOVA ($F_{(3, 13669)}$ = 197.320, P= < 0.0001). A Tukey post-hoc test revealed that the total pharmacy cost was statistically significantly higher among Indian ethnicity (RM 613.93, SD 98.41, P < 0.0001) and other ethnicity (RM 578.47, SD 144.51, P < 0.0001) compared to Malay ethnicity (RM 242.02, SD 65.37, P < 0.0001) and Chinese ethnicity (RM 214.66, SD 27.99, P < 0.0001) respectively.

There were no statistically significant differences between the Malay ethnicity and Chinese ethnicity (p = 0.269) and between Indian ethnicity and other ethnicity (p= 0.561), table 4.13.

Table 4.13 Ethnicity comparison to total pharmacy cost (ANOVA analysis of Trimmed data, n=13,673)

Ethnicity	Total Pharmacy Cost				
	N	Mean	SD	F.	*P
Malay	6,738	242.02	65.37	179.320	0.000
Chinese	3,801	214.66	27.95		
Indian	1,887	613.93	98.41		
Others	1,247	578.47	144.51		

*P Value Significant < 0.05

4.7.7 Association between Level of Severity and Total Pharmacy Cost

A one-way between-groups analysis of variance was conducted to explore the impact of ethnicity on the total pharmacy cost. Severity of illness was divided into three groups (group 1: severity levels I; group 2: severity level II; group 3: severity level III).

There was a statistically significant difference between groups as determined by one-way ANOVA ($F (2, 13670) = 1327.693$, P= < 0.0001). A Tukey post-hoc test revealed that the total pharmacy cost was statistically significantly higher among patients/ episodes in severity level III (RM 1,008.59, SD 157.23, $P < 0.0001$) and patients/ episodes in severity level II (RM 296.98, SD 49.28, $P < 0.0001$) compared to patients/episodes in severity level I (RM 126.05, SD 21.81, $P < 0.0001$).

There were statistically significant differences between the severity level III and severity level II (p < 0.0001), between severity level III and severity level I (p < 0.0001), and between severity level II and severity level I (p < 0.0001), table 4.14.

Table 4.14   Severity level comparison to total pharmacy cost (ANOVA analysis, n=13,673)

Severity level	Total Pharmacy Cost				
	N	Mean	SD	F.	*P
Severity level I	7,329	126.05	21.81	1327.693	0.000
Severity level II	4,210	296.98	49.28		
Severity level III	2,134	1,008.59	157.23		

*P Value Significant < 0.05

4.7.8   Association between all Independent Variables and the Total Inpatient Pharmacy Cost

Table 4.15 presents the zero-order correlation between the independent and the dependent variables in the multiple linear regression models. The total pharmacy cost was correlated with all independent variables at a p-value < 0.01 with exception of severity level 2 at p= <0.05.

Dummy variables have been prepared to be used in linear regression as follows: Type of cases (Surgical=1, Medical =0); Gender (Male=1, Female=0); Severity of illness (Level II= 1, Others=0); (Level III =1, Others =0); Ethnicity (Malay = 1, Others =0); (Chinese= 1, Others = 0) and (Indian =1, Others =0).

The correlation was positive with age (Pearson's r = 0.147), length of stay (Pearson's r = 0.502), number of items (Pearson's r = 0.376), gender (Pearson's r = 0.090), severity level III (Pearson's r =0.391), Indian ethnicity (Pearson's r = 0.156), surgical cases (Pearson's r = 0.050), while it was negative correlation with severity level II (Pearson's r = -0.017), Malay (Pearson's r = -0.096) and Chinese (Pearson's r = -0.083) ethnicities at a p-value < 0.01.

Age has highly positive correlation with severity level III (Pearson's r =0.256, p< 0.01) compared to other variables where the correlation was marginal or no correlation such as in Chinese ethnicity variable. Length of stay was correlated with all variables, however the high positive correlation was with number of items (Pearson's r =0.630, p<0.01) and severity level III (Pearson's r =0.335, p< 0.01) respectively.

Although the number of items has no correlation with severity level II (Pearson's r = -0.004), the highest positive correlation was with severity level III (Pearson's r =0.258, p<0.01) compared to marginal correlations with other variables.

Severity level II was noted to have marginal correlation with most of variables compared to level III which has high positive correlation with most of variables. Surgical cases have a positive and marginally correlation with almost all variables. All ethnicity groups negatively correlated with each other.

Development of Pharmacy Service Weights in the Implementation of Casemix System for Provider Payment

Table 4.15 Zero-order correlation between socio demographic, clinical and total pharmacy cost (n= 13,673)

	Age	LOS	No. of items	Surgical	Males	Severity L II	Severity L III	Malay	Chinese	Indian
Age	1	0.176**	0.155**	-0.127**	0.112**	0.102**	0.256**	-0.021*	-0.016	0.072**
LOS	0.176**	1	0.630**	-0.058**	0.109**	0.021*	0.335**	-0.057**	-0.086**	0.110**
No. of items	0.155**	0.630**	1	-0.062**	0.100**	-0.004	0.258**	-0.030**	-0.049**	0.079**
Surgical	0.127**	0.058**	0.062**	1	0.090**	0.035**	0.169**	0.043**	0.006	0.031**
Males	0.112**	0.109**	0.100**	-0.090**	1	0.002	0.095**	-0.034**	0.005	0.024**
Severity LII	0.102**	0.021*	-0.004	-0.035**	0.002	1	-0.237**	0.000	0.007	0.024**
Severity LIII	0.256**	0.335**	0.258**	-0.169**	0.095**	-0.287**	1	-0.091**	-0.034**	0.142**
Malay	-0.021*	-0.057**	-0.030**	0.043**	-0.034**	0.000	-0.091**	1	-0.612**	-0.394**
Chinese	-0.016	-0.068**	-0.049**	-0.006	0.005	0.007	-0.034**	-0.612**	1	-0.248**
Indian	0.072**	0.110**	0.079**	-0.031**	0.024**	0.024**	0.142**	-0.394**	-0.248**	1
Total pharmacy cost	0.147**	0.502**	0.376**	-0.056**	0.090**	-0.017	0.391**	-0.096**	-0.083**	0.156**

*$P < 0.05$, **$P< 0.01$, Type of cases (Surgical=1, Medical =0), Gender (Male=1, Female=0), Severity of illness (Level II= 1, Others=0), (Level III =1, Others =0), Ethnicity (Malay = 1, Others =0), (Chinese= 1, Others =-), (Indian =1, Others =0)

4.8 MULTIVARIATE LINEAR REGRESSION ANALYSIS

A multivariate linear regression model was run to predict the factors influencing the total pharmacy cos. All variable were included in the multivariate analysis.

4.8.1 Regression Model Fitness

Table 4.16 presents the model summery of a number of values including R value (the multiple correlation coefficients) which is considered to be one measure of the quality of the prediction of the dependent variable.

A value of 0.572, in this study, indicates a good level of prediction. The R^2 value (the coefficient of determination), which is the proportion of variance in the dependent variable that can be explained by the independent variables. The R^2 is 0.327. This means that the independent variables explain 32.7% of the variation in the dependent variable.

Table 4.16 Model summary of linear regression Model

Model	R	R Square	Adjusted R Square	Std. Error of the Estimate
1	0.572	0.327	0.326	625.16858

4.8.2 Statistical Significance

The *F*-ratio in the **ANOVA** table 4.17 tests whether the overall regression model is a good fit for the data. The table shows that the independent variables are jointly statistically significant to predict the dependent variable, $F(8, 13664) = 829.328$, $p < .0005$ (i.e., the regression model is a good fit of the data).

Table 4.17 ANOVA test to examine the fitness of model for (the trimmed data, n=13,673)

Model	Sum of Squares	df	Mean Square	F	Sig.
Regression	2.593E9	8	3.241E8	829.328	0.000
Residual	5.340E9	13664	390835.757		
Total	7.933E9	13672			

4.8.3 Estimated Model Coefficients

Table 4.18 presents the coefficients with t-value and corresponding p-value of all variable with exception of age and Indian ethnicity were excluded because of coefficients were statistically insignificant. After examining the eight independent statistically significant coefficients variables in table 4.18 the prediction equation and its interpretation is based on the unstandardized coefficients, as follows:

Total Pharmacy Cost = 1.381 + (37.12 x Length of Stay) + (10.55 x Number of Items) + (31.43 x Surgical Cases) + (28.38 x Males) + (82.88 x Severity level II) + (531.75 x Severity level III) – (193.99 x Malay Ethnicity) – (212.12 Chinese Ethnicity).

4.8.4 Interpretation of Regression Model Equation

The Constant is the predicted value of the dependent variable when all of the independent variables have a value of zero.

In the context of this analysis, the predicted total pharmacy cost for zero length of stay and zero number of items, zero surgical cases, zero gender (males), zero Severity level II, zero Severity level III, zero Malay ethnicity and zero Chinese ethnicity is 1.381.

The slope of length of stay is 37.118. This means that for every one unit (day of stay) increase in length of stay, predicted total pharmacy cost increase by 37.118 units (RM), after controlling for number of items, surgical cases, gender (males), severity level II, severity level III, Malay ethnicity and Chinese ethnicity. Then hereby the null hypothesis that mentioned "patients who have the longer length of stay in the hospital are more likely to have high total pharmacy cost" is confirmed.

The slope of number of items is 10.553. This means that for every one unit (item of drug or supplies) increase in number of items, predicted total pharmacy cost increase by 10.553 units (RM), after controlling for length of stay, surgical cases, gender (males), severity level II, severity level III, Malay ethnicity and Chinese ethnicity. Then hereby the null hypothesis that mentioned "Patients who have more items of prescribed drugs and supplies items are more likely to have high total pharmacy cost" is confirmed.

The slope of surgical cases is 31.432. This means that for every one unit (surgical procedure) increase in surgical cases, predicted total pharmacy cost increase by 31.432 units (RM), after controlling for length of stay, number of items, gender (males), severity level II, severity level III, Malay ethnicity and Chinese ethnicity. Then hereby the null hypothesis that mentioned "patients who have undergone more complex procedures (surgical case) are more likely to have total pharmacy cost" is confirmed.

The slope of gender is 28.378. This means that for every one unit (male) increase in number of gender, predicted total pharmacy cost increase by 28.378 units (RM), after controlling for length of stay, surgical cases, severity level II, severity level III, Malay ethnicity and Chinese ethnicity. Then herby the null hypothesis that mentioned "Male patients are more likely to have high total pharmacy cost than female patients" is confirmed.

The slope of severity level II is 82.778. This means that for every one unit (patient suffers from minor complications with a second diagnosis and co morbidity that prolong the length of patient's stay by one day) increase in severity level II, predicted total pharmacy cost increase by 82.778 units (RM), after controlling for length of stay, number of items, surgical cases, gender (males), Severity level III, Malay ethnicity and Chinese ethnicity. Then hereby the null hypothesis that mentioned "Patients who have higher level of severity are more likely to have high total pharmacy cost" is confirmed.

The slope of severity level III is 531.750. This means that for every one unit (the patient had a major complication and co morbidity that prolonged the inpatient stay by at least two to three days) increase in severity level III, predicted total pharmacy cost increase by 531.750 units (RM), after controlling for length of stay, number of items, surgical cases, gender (males), severity level II, Malay ethnicity and Chinese ethnicity. Then hereby the null hypothesis that mentioned "Patients who have higher level of severity are more likely to have high total pharmacy cost" is confirmed.

The slope of Malay ethnicity is -193.938. This means that, on average, predicted reading scores for other ethnicity are 193.938 points lower than for Malay ethnicity, after controlling for length of stay, number of items, surgical cases, gender (males), severity level II, severity level III, and Chinese ethnicity.

The slope of Chinese ethnicity is -212.117. This means that, on average, predicted reading scores for other ethnicity are 212.117 points lower than for Chinese ethnicity, after controlling for length of stay, number of items, surgical cases, gender (males), severity level II, severity level III, and Malay ethnicity.

Table 4.18 Multivariate linear regression coefficients results

Model	Unstandardized Coefficients B	Std. Error	Standardized Coefficients Beta	t	Sig.
(Constant)	1.381	16.112		0.086	0.932
Length Of Stay	37.118	0.998	**0.349**	37.199	0.000
No. of items	10.553	1.188	0.081	8.879	0.000
Surgical cases	31.432	11.253	0.020	2.793	0.005
Gender (males)	28.378	10.954	0.018	2.591	0.010
Severity Level II	82.778	12.246	0.050	6.760	0.000
Severity Level III	531.750	16.861	**0.253**	31.536	0.000
Malay ethnicity	- 193.938-	13.714	- 0.127-	-14.141-	0.000
Chinese ethnicity	- 212.117-	15.260	- 0.125-	-13.901-	0.000

4.9 DEVELOPMENT OF CASEMIX PHARMACY IN-PATIENT SERVICE WEIGHTS

As a result of data trimming and excluding the MY-DRGs with less than 5 cases, over 450 MY-DRGs identified in the study, 5.6% of which had only 5 cases. DRG O-6-13-I, Vaginal Delivery with severity level one (5.0%) was the highest volume DRG identified in this study with 688 cases. Out of 32 Casemix Major Groups (CMG) codes and description used in MY-DRG, 21 (65.63%) have been used. The highest volume 2,363 (17.28%) was the Deliveries Groups (O). The lowest volume 6 (0.04%) was the Substance abuse & dependence Groups (T). Five of CMG namely: Deliveries Groups (O), Cardiovascular system

Groups (I), Digestive system Groups (K), Musculoskeletal system & connective tissue Groups (M), Female reproductive system Groups (W) contributed to approximately 7,355 (53.79%) of total CMG assignment, table 4.19.

Table 4.19 Casemix Major Groups (CMG) codes and description used in MY-DRG (n= 13,673)

No.	CMG Codes	Description	N	%
1	A	Infectious & parasitic diseases Groups	361	2.64
2	B	Hepatobiliary & pancreatic system Groups	328	2.40
3	C	Myeloproliferative system & neoplasms Groups	202	1.48
4	D	Haemopoeitic & immune system Groups	181	1.32
5	E	Endocrine system, nutrition & metabolism Groups	327	2.39
6	F	Mental Health and Behavioral Groups	354	2.59
7	G	Central nervous system Groups	757	5.54
8	H	Eye and Adnexa Groups	414	3.03
9	I	Cardiovascular system Groups	1,325	9.69
10	J	Respiratory system Groups	996	7.28
11	K	Digestive system Groups	1,315	9.62
12	L	Skin, subcutaneous tissue & breast Groups	649	4.75
13	M	Musculoskeletal system & connective tissue Groups	1,206	8.82
14	N	Nephro-urinary System Groups	690	5.05
15	O	Deliveries Groups	2,363	17.28
16	S	Injuries, poisonings & toxic effects of drugs Groups	98	0.72
17	T	Substance abuse & dependence Groups	6	0.04
18	U	Ear, nose, mouth & throat Groups	697	5.10
19	V	Male reproductive System Groups	211	1.54
20	W	Female reproductive system Groups	1,146	8.38
21	Z	Factors influencing health status & other contacts with health services Groups	47	0.34
		Total	13,673	100.00

Average pharmacy cost of the 450 MY-DRGs was 484.48. MY-DRG F-4-16-III, Dementia and Other Organic Brain Disturbances Including Mental Retardation with severity level III was the closest average (RM486.08) among all other MY-DRGs. Thus this average was the base (denominator) used in the question to estimate the pharmacy service weights for all other MY-DRGs.

Tables 4.20 and table 4.21 show the pharmacy service weights of the highest and lowest 20 MY-DRGs respectively. MY-DRG casemix group of Lymphoma & Chronic Leukemia group with severity level three (C-4-11-III) has the highest pharmacy service weight of 11.8 equivalents to average pharmacy cost of (RM 5,383.90).

While the MY-DRG casemix group for Circumcision with severity level one (V-1-15-I) has the lowest pharmacy service weight of 0.04 equivalents to average pharmacy cost (RM17.83). Appendix 3 presents the pharmacy service weights of the total 450 MY-DRGs identified in this study.

4.10 CONCLUSION

In conclusion, applying of mixed approach of step-down and bottom-up costing methodology indicated that the drugs and supplies were the highest component of inpatient pharmacy cost. Furthermore, the multiple linear regression models showed that the increase in the hospitalization period accompanied with a major complication and co-morbidity had the highest influence on the total pharmacy cost. MY-DRG casemix group of Lymphoma & Chronic Leukemia group with severity level three (C-4-11-III) has the highest pharmacy service weight of 11.8 equivalents to average pharmacy cost of (RM 5,383.90).

Development of Pharmacy Service Weights in the Implementation of Casemix System for Provider Payment

Table 4.20 Pharmacy in-patient service weights of the highest 20 MY-DRGs.

No.	MY-DRG	No. of Episodes Per DRG	Total Pharmacy Cost per DRG	Average Pharmacy Cost per DRG	Pharmacy Service Weight
1	C-4-11-III	38	204,588.16	5,383.90	11.08
2	B-1-10-III	11	49,817.84	4,528.89	9.32
3	J-1-20-III	5	22,178.34	4,435.67	9.13
4	U-1-20-III	17	61,664.92	3,627.35	7.46
5	M-1-20-III	5	16,848.74	3,369.75	6.93
6	C-4-10-III	31	104,232.86	3,362.35	6.92
7	G-1-11-III	14	46,170.40	3,297.89	6.78
8	M-1-60-III	8	22,978.67	2,872.33	5.91
9	S-4-13-III	6	17,148.36	2,858.06	5.88
10	D-4-10-III	13	34,282.24	2,637.10	5.43
11	B-1-11-III	7	18,080.84	2,582.98	5.31
12	M-1-03-III	11	26,994.90	2,454.08	5.05
13	J-4-12-III	9	20,444.37	2,271.60	4.67
14	G-4-21-III	5	10,925.50	2,185.10	4.50
15	D-1-10-I	9	18,569.22	2,063.25	4.24
16	I-4-13-III	6	11,693.31	1,948.89	4.01
17	I-1-04-III	5	9,550.77	1,910.15	3.93
18	D-1-20-III	5	9,455.59	1,891.12	3.89
19	K-1-20-III	16	30,134.09	1,883.38	3.87
20	I-4-14-III	10	18,375.21	1,837.52	3.78

Table 4.21 Pharmacy in-patient service weights of the lowest 20 MY-DRGs.

No.	MY-DRG	No. of Episodes Per DRG	Total Pharmacy Cost per DRG	Average Pharmacy Cost per DRG	Pharmacy Service Weight
1	N-4-15-I	15	859.26	57.28	0.12
2	W-4-14-I	39	2,181.90	55.95	0.12
3	V-1-11-I	7	371.15	53.02	0.11
4	U-4-14-I	80	4,207.47	52.59	0.11
5	A-4-12-I	7	363.18	51.88	0.11
6	I-4-17-I	9	448.96	49.88	0.10
7	W-4-14-II	40	1,964.24	49.11	0.10
8	N-1-12-I	11	527.88	47.99	0.10
9	U-4-11-I	8	372.16	46.52	0.10
10	A-4-12-II	7	321.54	45.93	0.09
11	J-4-13-I	5	228.51	45.70	0.09
12	G-4-16-I	7	313.50	44.79	0.09
13	W-4-15-I	11	473.64	43.06	0.09
14	U-4-12-I	6	231.91	38.65	0.08
15	K-1-14-I	54	1,942.32	35.97	0.07
16	W-1-11-I	141	4,426.79	31.40	0.06
17	K-4-17-I	117	3,625.94	30.99	0.06
18	G-4-25-I	18	533.33	29.63	0.06
19	W-4-13-I	23	637.16	27.70	0.06
20	V-1-15-I	25	438.28	17.53	0.04

CHAPTER V

DISCUSSION

5.1 INTRODUCTION

In this chapter, costing methodology, total inpatient pharmacy cost, predictors of the total pharmacy cost and development of casemix pharmacy service weight would be discussed.

5.2 COSTING METHODOLOGY

The main objective of this study was to develop the MY-DRG casemix inpatient pharmacy service weights in UKM Medical Centre. For this purpose a mixed approach of top-down and bottom-up costing methodology has been recruited jointly (Vander Plaetse et al. 2005; Tsilaajav 2009; Hendriks; Mogyorosy & Smith 2005; Shepard et al. 2000). Although international literature indicated that there are several approaches to estimate the cost of providing services by health related institution including hospitals. However, there is no unique, appropriate and acceptable methodology for costing hospital services (Mogyorosy & Smith 2005).

Type of the service and reason for costing in addition to economical feasibility of cost calculation are the main determinants for selection of appropriate costing approach. Thus, the cost of a particular service can vary substantially according to the purpose of cost data for which it was generated (Zimmerman 2003). Data was retrospectively obtained from the pharmacy electronic prescription system and the casemix database as well as hospital information support system in UKM Medical Centre.

Zhao and his colleagues (2005) indicted that the pharmacy cost is specifically predictable from the drugs data compared to other medical cost and total hospital cost which could be predicted from the diagnoses data. However, they concluded that the total health care costs could be predicted better using combination of drug and diagnostic data than either type of data alone (Zhao et al. 2005).

This study indicated that the drugs and supplies made the highest component of the pharmacy cost. These findings come in line with other international and local studies considering the pharmacy services as ancillary services (Duckett 1998) and among the highest components of cost in the hospital (Heslop 2012; Mills et al. 1993; Vander Plaetse et al. 2005; Centers for Medicare and Medicaid Services 2011).

Study done by Riewpaiboon et al. (2005) in Thailand aimed to explore cost structure of pharmacy department and propose more appropriate reimbursement method. This study revealed that the drug cost (acquisition cost) accounted for 77% of the total pharmacy cost with the highest contribution 96% from the direct cost compared to 4% of the indirect cost. To our knowledge, the pharmacy services and its related weights are commonly studied within the general hospital level costing and are rarely to be evaluated as an independent subject (Duckett 1998; Tsilaajav 2009).

In 2004, two studies done in UKMMC, and the costing analysis were conducted based on the casemix concept of the top-down costing approach. The first one was to study the cost analysis for cardiology. This study found that the three biggest components of medical cardiology cases are ICU cost (38.0%), pharmacy component (14.2%) and ward services (12.7%). In the surgical cardiology, the biggest component of cost was the operation theatre (27.9%), followed by ward services (25.4%) and pharmacy component (8.5%) (Amrizal et al.2005).

The other study was the cost analysis and cost weight for the treatment of orthopedic cases in HUKM. This study showed that the top three components of cost for the treatment of medical orthopedic was pharmacy services (22.3%), followed by ward services which was (20.7%) and laboratory services which was (12.1%), while the top three components of cost for treatment of surgical orthopedic was operating theatre services which was (21.2%), followed by Pharmacy Services which was (17.6%) and ward services which was (16.3). It is noted that for both the medical and surgical partitions of cardiology and orthopedic cases, the pharmacy component services were among the top three contributors of the larger portion of cost or resources (Rohaizat et al. 2005).

Nor Azlin et al. 2012 conducted study in UKMMC aimed to estimate cost of inpatient medical care due to stroke using a top-down costing approach. This study revealed that the human resources made up the highest cost component (36% of the total cost), followed by medications (23.5% of the total cost) and laboratory services (9.2% of the total cost).

Study done by Vander Plaetse et al. (2005) to generate data on the cost and revenue of health care delivered in a rural Zimbabwean district was based on a combination of step-down cost accounting and detailed observation of resource use at the point of service. This study found that 54% of total costs for the district were for salaries, 20% for drugs, 11% for equipment and buildings (including depreciation) and 15% for other costs.

However, Mills et al. (1993) found a strikingly low proportion of district recurrent costs were absorbed by salaries and wages (27-39%, depending on the district) and a surprisingly high proportion by drugs and medical supplies (24-37%). Also when the costs have been distributed by cost centre in four Malawi district hospitals, the pharmacy was the most costly department, absorbing 25-38% of total recurrent costs compared to other centers such as administration accounted for 5-9% and maintenance for fewer than 4%.

In a costing study of national rural health services in Indonesia, Berman et al. (1989) reported that if all programmes are combined together, the greatest proportion (approximately 81%) of total costs belong to staff, drugs and supplies components. However, if the cost components are analyzed separately, the contribution of drugs and supplies alone ranged from 43.3% of the total costs for curative care to 8.3% of other programmes such as the extension activities.

Costing study done in Philippine for selected hospitals used both the activity based and step-down costing approaches found that medicines and supplies cost contributed to more than 25% of the total hospital cost (Tsilaajav 2009).

Another local study conducted by Suhil et al. (2010) in Universiti Sains Malaysia Medical center aimed to evaluate the direct medical cost in treating hypertension in a Malaysian public university. This study found that the drugs constituted about 74.6% of total direct medical costs in 2005 and 80.5% of total direct medical costs in 2006, while the cost of health personnel constituted 25.3% of the total direct medical cost in 2005 and 19.4% of total direct medical costs in 2006.

5.3 PREDICTORS OF THE TOTAL INPATIENT PHARMACY COST

A multiple linear regression model was run to predict the total inpatient pharmacy cost from a combination of socio demographic data such as (age, gender, and ethnicity); drug data such as (the number of medications and supplies items prescribed in each episode of care); and the diagnostic data such as (the length of stay, type of the cases and the level of severity of illness).

These independent variables were found significant predictors of pharmacy and other medical cost in several previous studies (Zhao et al. 2005; Van Vliet 1992; Wouters1991; Wrobel et al. 2003; Coulsen et al. 1992; Nikkel et al 2012; Andayani et al. 2010; Berman et al. 1989; Aljunid et al. 2007; Chow et al. 2010).

Age and Indian ethnicity were excluded because of coefficients were statistically insignificant. Length of stay, number of items, surgical cases, males, severity level II, severity level III, Malay and Chinese ethnicities variables were statistically significantly predicted the total pharmacy cost $F(8, 13664) = 829.328$, $P < 0.0005$, while $R^2 = 0.327$ which means that the independent variables explain 32.7% of the variation in the dependent variable. All independent variables added statistically significant to the prediction, < 0.05.

Length of stay (B = 0.349, P < 0.0005) and severity level III (B = 0.253, P < 0.0005) appear to be the strongest predictors for the total pharmacy cost; followed by the number of items (B = 0.081, P < 0.0005) and severity level II (B = 0.050, P = <0.0005). The more complicated cases, the longer the length of stay, the more drugs and supplies were prescribed, the more staff cost, the more pharmacy use of the overhead cost centre allocation, the higher is the total pharmacy cost.

In fact, comparison to similar findings was difficult as most studies tend to correlate the predicting factors including the length of stay, level of severity and prescribed drugs and supplies with total hospital cost or drug cost not the total pharmacy cost alone.

Chow et al. (2010) and his colleagues examined the factors influencing the cost of acute stroke care in Singapore. They found that the length of stay is strongly correlated to the total cost and significantly incurred higher total cost in multivariate analysis. Another more recent Singaporean study conducted in single center revealed that the longer length of stay and severe sepsis were associated with a higher total hospital cost for management of lymphoma patients with chemotherapy-induced febrile neutropenia (FN) and the main cost drivers were the medication costs and ward costs (Wang 2014).

Bahadori et al. (2009) reviewed about sixty-eight publications to determine the burden of disease costs associated with asthma. He concluded that the hospitalization and medications was the most important cost driver of direct costs. At the same time, the strategy of reducing the length of hospitalization has saved considerably on hospital cost (Carey 2003). Cortoos et al. (2013) reported that the most important driver of hospital costs associated with Community-acquired pneumonia (CAP) was the time between clinical stability and actual hospital discharge. The length of stay after clinical stability and time to clinical stability had the highest influence on the total cost.

Other important predictor for inpatient total pharmacy cost is the level of severity. Patient with a major complication and co-morbidity usually accompanied with longer length of stay and most probably need high professional consultancy with more and may be higher generation of drugs being prescribed.

Nikkel et al. (2012) indicated that cost of hospitalization and length of stay are affected significantly by presence of co-morbidities following hip fractures in older Americans. Nor Azlin et al. (2012) found that the LOS and cost of care varied across different stroke severity levels ($p < 0.01$). Gordon et al. 2012 indicated that Pharmacy, ambulatory, and inpatient care collectively accounted for 90% of non cirrhotic liver disease (NCD) cost and this proportion increased with severity. Furthermore, the prevention of complications would potentially reduce the healthcare expenditure (Andayani et al. 2010).

Edwards et al (1991) found that the increase in drugs cost was the consequence of a general increase in prescribed items throughout the major therapeutic groups. The more drugs were prescribed, the higher is the drug cost (Aljunid et al. 2007).

Many factors affect the level of a population's drug consumption,' but its demographic structure is undoubtedly one of the most influential (Roberts & Harris 1993). Bramkamp et al. (2007) indicated that the costs of acute coronary syndromes (ACS) in Switzerland were independently influenced by age, gender and existent co-morbidities. On the other hand the Canadian Institute for Health Information (2012) indicated that the aging of the Canadian population from 1998 to 2007 caused pharmaceutical spending to grow by approximately 1.0% per year.

On average, older Canadians spend significantly more than their younger counterparts. Peiró et al. (2004) Indicated that the longer length of stay, the presence of aggressiveness /agitation, a diagnosis of schizophrenia, age younger than 25 years and the use of atypical antipsychotics were associated with higher costs in antipsychotic drug treatment.

The multiple linear regression model predict that the patients who stayed longer, with high severity of illness, increased number of prescribed drugs and supplies items, having surgical procedures, being male from other ethnicity are more likely to have high influence on the total inpatient pharmacy cost.

The findings of this study are supported by similar outcomes from some other studies conducted in different Malaysian medical centers, for example, study conducted by Aljunid et al. (2007) in UKM Medical center indicated that the frequency of prescriptions for cardiovascular drugs for men was higher than that for women. The number of drugs was observed to be higher in patients aged older than 60 years old, length of stay longer than seven days and the presence of co-morbidities and complications during hospitalization.

Another study conducted by Dahlui et al. (2012) aimed to determine the actual costs of health care service provision, at the University of Malaya Medical Centre (UMMC) for the calendar year 2010. The study applied a top-down method and step-down allocation of overhead costs to the final health care departments. This study found that the major cost component for the medical wards was for consumables which made up 70% of the total cost for the medical inpatient services. In contrast, costs for treatment procedures made up 62% of total costs for the surgical inpatient services. Severity of illness was identified as the main risk factor for readmission in the same medical centre (Amer Siddiq et al. 2008).

5.4 DEVELOPMENT OF CASEMIX PHARMACY SERVICE WEIGHT

Table 4.20 reported that the MY-DRG case-mix group of Lymphoma & Chronic Leukemia group with severity level III (C-4-11-III) has the highest pharmacy service weight of 11.08 equivalents to average pharmacy cost of RM 5383.90.

While the MY-DRG casemix group for Circumcision with severity level I (V-1-15-I) has the lowest pharmacy service weight of 0.04

equivalents to average pharmacy cost of RM 17.83. This means that a lymphoma & chronic leukemia patient/ episode is on average 11.08 times more expensive inpatient pharmacy cost than the average cost of all patients / episodes in MY-DRG in 2011. Service weights are a reflection that different cases not only in cost differing amounts, but utilize differing amounts of resources in the different areas within department or hospitals (Botz 1989; James 2005; Langenbrunner et al. 2009; Heslop 2012).

In fact two of Casemix Major Groups (Myeloproliferative system & neoplasms Groups) namely: MY-DRG case-mix group of Lymphoma & Chronic Leukemia group with severity level three (C-4-11-III) and MY-DRG case-mix group of Acute Leukemia group with severity level three (C-4-10-III) were among the first ten highest pharmacy service weight groups.

It is not surprising because even in term of generic alternatives the prices of cancer medicines are high compared with those for nonmalignant diseases (Siddiqui & Rajkumar 2012). On the other hand, in Malaysia about 5% of the gross domestic product (GDP) has been spent on healthcare and about 98% of cost of public health services including cancer medications was funded directly by government (Hassali et al. 2013; Keat & Ghani 2013). Public health care services are funded through general taxation, with annual health budgets allocated by Ministry of Finance to the Ministry of Health. The proportion of general revenue allocated for Ministry of Health functions in the National Budget is decided annually (Chua & Cheah 2012)

Ezat et al. (2013) conducted an economic evaluation study in UKMMC to determine the cost of colorectal cancer (CRC) management. On average the Cost of treating a case of colorectal cancer in stage I is RM13, 623, stage II is RM19, 753, stage III RM24, 972 and stage IV is RM27, 163. This study also indicated that the cost of CRC management increase with the increasing stage of the disease (Kruskal Wallis, $X^2=106$, $p<0.001$).

Wang et al. (2014) reported that the cost for management of lymphoma patients with chemotherapy-induced febrile neutropenia

(FN) was associated with the longer length of stay and severe sepsis among Singaporean patient. Ko et al. (2014) indicated that drug-related hospitalization among cancer patients is costly. Longer LOS was found to be correlated (r = 0.86, P < 0.001) with higher direct medical costs.

Additionally, an important finding noticed in table 4.20, was among the highest ten inpatient pharmacy service weights in UKMMC there is six surgical procedures with severity level III: MY-DRG case-mix group of PANCREAS & LIVER OPERATIONS group with severity level three (B-1-10-III); MY-DRG case-mix group of SIMPLE RESPIRATORY SYSTEM OPERATIONS group with severity level three (J-1-20-III); MY-DRG case-mix group of OTHER EAR NOSE MOUTH & THROAT OPERATIONS group with severity level three (U-1-20-III); MY-DRG case-mix group of HIP & FEMUR OPERATION EXCLUDING JOINTS group with severity level three (M-1-20-III); MY-DRG case-mix group of VENTRICULAR SHUNT group with severity level three (G-1-11-III); MY-DRG case-mix group of OTHER OPERATIONS OF MUSCULOSKELETEL SYSTEM & CONNECTIVE TISSUE group with severity level three (M-1-60-III), in addition to one group related to complications of treatment & procedures: MY-DRG case-mix group of COMPLICATIONS OF TREATMENT & PROCEDURES group with severity level three (S-4-13-III).

Healthcare cost and resource utilization were strongly associated with postoperative complications and primarily driven by differences in the cost of the index hospitalization. At the same, the reducing morbidity after the surgical procedures may substantially reduce hospital costs and increase the efficiency of resource utilization (Nathan et al. 2014; Vaughan-Sarrazin et al. 2011; Khan et al. 2011).

Khan et al. (2011) in his study assessed the association of clinically important postoperative complications with total hospital costs and length of stay (LOS) in patients undergoing noncardiac surgery indicted that postoperative complications increased hospital costs by 78% (95% confidence interval [CI]: 68% to 90%) and LOS by 114% (95% CI: 100% to 130%) after adjustment for patient preoperative and surgical characteristics.

Recently Zoucas & Lydrup (2014) assessed the impact of surgical complications on healthcare resource utilization for patients undergoing elective colorectal procedures. They indicated that occurrence of any complication at index admission increased total hospital costs 2.1fold (EUR 25,680 vs. EUR 12,405). These increases were primarily due to prolonged hospitalization and intensive care unit (ICU) expenditures. Also, hospital costs were significantly increased by any postoperative complications, reoperations, high complexity of surgical procedures and high co-morbidity index.

Indeed, in our study about 38.1% of patients were admitted with a principle diagnosis as surgical procedure. It was not surprising, because the UKM Medical Centre provides a broad range of teaching and tertiary referral services in addition to the oncology unit and the primary emergency reception centre for the South Eastern suburbs of Kuala Lumpur, the capital city of Malaysia. This may explain partly the volume of surgical procedures carried on there. However, Nathan et al. 2014 indicated that the complication rates were not correlated with hospital volume, but occurrence of complications was associated with 47% to 70% higher costs.

CHAPTER VI
CONCLUSION AND RECOMMENDATION

6.1 CONCLUSION

A mixed approach which is based partly on top-down and partly on bottom up costing methodology has been recruited to develop MY-DRG case-mix inpatient pharmacy service weight for 450 groups utilized by the UKMMC in 2011. This methodology can be used for calculating pharmacy service weight among government hospital such as general, district and private hospital in future. It is a hope that the results of this study will participate in the development of MY-DRG in UKMMC specifically in pharmacy services.

Knowing which DRG consumes the bulk of the resources would greatly support decision makers regarding budget planning of pharmacy services and patients' outcomes, and eventually will contribute in the quality of care and services improvement as well as an effective use of resources in UKMMC.

This study also showed that using of combination of e-prescription data and casemix database would greatly facilitate the activity based costing methodology to estimate the pharmacy service weight by identifying pharmacy services and the actual cost of care.

In fact, the availability of pharmacy service weights or cost weights will enable a comparison is made between the treatments cost of various DRG cases within and between hospitals (James 2005). For the purpose of using DRG as a base of hospital payment, a price needs to be assigned to each DRG. This is usually done by assigning a cost relativity (or service weight) with a base price multiplier (Luce 1996).

A multiple linear regression was run to predict the total pharmacy cost from gender, age, ethnicity, type of cases, severity of illness, length of stay and number of drugs and supplies items prescribed in each episode of care. Age and Indian ethnicity were excluded because of coefficients were statistically insignificant.

Length of stay, number of items, surgical cases, males, severity level II, severity level III, Malay and Chinese ethnicities variables statistically significantly predicted the total pharmacy cost F (8, 13,664) = 829.328, $P < 0.0005$, while $R^2 = 0.327$ which means that the independent variables explain 32.7% of the variation in the dependent variable. All independent variables added statistically significant to the prediction, < 0.05.

Length of stay (B = 0.349, P <0.0005) and severity level III (B = 0.253, P < 0.0005) appear to be the strongest predictors of the total pharmacy cost; followed by the number of items (B = 0.081, P< 0.0005), severity level II (B = 0.050, P = <0.0005), surgical cases (B = 0.020, P = 0.005) and males (B = 0.018, P = 0.010) respectively. Patients from the Malay and Chinese ethnicity are the less likely to contribute more to the total pharmacy cost compared to other ethnicity.

In conclusion, while it was not possible to capture all of the factors that could predict the total pharmacy cost, in general, the patients who stayed longer, with high severity of illness, increased number of prescribed drugs and supplies items, having surgical procedures, being male from other ethnicity are more likely to have high influence on the total inpatient pharmacy cost.

6.2 LIMITATION OF STUDY

This study has few areas of limitations. First of all, this study was not designed to cover a representative size of hospitals in Malaysia due to time and resource constraints in addition to the limited number of hospitals that implemented DRG system in Malaysia. Other limitation is related to (date) of e-prescription issue which was not always be the same date of patient admission. This limitation made the joining of e-prescription data to casemix data to be done manually.

6.3 RECOMMENDATIONS

This study used the electronic prescription jointly with casemix database to calculate the total pharmacy cost and to develop the inpatient pharmacy service weight in UKM Medical Centre. The process of joining data from e-prescription system to its counterpart in casemix data base depends on two factors; medical record number (MRN) and date of e-prescription from prescription system, while the factors used from casemix data base were the MRN and date of admission. Unfortunately, the date of prescription was not always the same date of admission. Therefore, the joining process has been done manually rather than to be electronically, thus we recommend:

a. Including the date of admission in each e-prescription which suppose to be the same date used in casemix data base.
b. Data-base of e-prescription should be linked to each episode of admission and out-patient visit for easier tracing.
c. Use the output of the study to indentify levels of efficiency of pharmacy services.
d. Regular monitoring of pharmacy cost to reduce wastages.
e. Further research to develop the outpatient pharmacy service weights.
f. Further research on other cost-weights such as ICU and other support services.

REFERENCES

Andayani, T.M., Ibrahim, M.I.M. & Asdie, A.H. 2010. Assessing the impact of complications on the direct medical costs of type 2 diabetes mellitus outpatients. *International Journal of Current Pharmaceutical Research* **2** (20): 32-35.

Aguado, A., Guinó, E., Mukherjee, B., Sicras, A., Serrat, J., Acedo, M., Ferro, J.J. & Moreno, V. 2008. Variability in prescription drug expenditures explained by adjusted clinical groups (ACG) case-mix: A cross-sectional study of patient electronic records in primary care. BMC *Health Services Research* **8**:53 (Online) http://www.biomedcentral.com/1472-6963/8/53 (29 March 2013).

Aisbett, C., Wiley, M., McCarthy, B. & Mulligan, A. 2007. Measuring hospital case mix: Evaluation of alternative approaches for the Irish hospital system, Working Paper, The Economic and Social Research Institute (ESRI), Dublin, No. 192, (Online) http://hdl.handle.net/10419/68019 (11March 2013).

Aljunid, S.M., Hamzah, S.M., Mutalib, S.A., Amrizal, M, N., Shafie, N. & Sulong, S. 2011. The UNU-CBGs: development and deployment of a real international open source Case-mix grouper for resource challenged countries, 27th Patient Classification Systems International (PCSI) Working Conference Montreal, Canada. 19-22 October 2011. (Abstract online) http://www.ncbi.nlm.nih.gov/pmc/articles/PMC3238203/ (5 February 2013).

Al-Junid, S.M., Sharifa Ezat, W.P, & Surianti, S. 2007. Prescribing patterns and drug cost among cardiovascular patients in Hospital Universiti Kebangsaan Malaysia. *Med J Malaysia* **62** (1): 59-65.

Amer Siddiq AN, NG CG, Aida SA, Zuraida NZ, Abdul Kadir R. 2008. Factors Affecting Readmission in A Teaching Hospital in Malaysia. MJP Ejournal**17**(1):

Amrizal MN, Rohaizat Y, Zafar A, Saperi, Syed A: Case-mix costing in Universiti Kebangsaan Malaysia hospital a top-down approach: cost analysis for cardiology cases. *MJPHM* 2005, **5**(Supplement 2): 33-44. (Online) http://www.mjphm.org.my/mjphm/journals/Volume%205%20%28Sup%202%29%20:%202005/Part%201.pdf (18 February 2013).

APDRG Suisse (2003) Cost Weights version 4.1. Institut de Santé et d'Economie Prilly, Switzerland, available at: http://www.apdrgsuisse.ch/public/fr/o_rapport_cw_v41_e.pdf.

Averill, R.F., Muldoon, J.H., Vertrees, J.C., Goldfield, N.I., Mullin, R.L., Fineran, E.C., Zhang, M.Z., Steinbeck, B. & Grant, T. 1998. The Evolution of Case Mix Measurement Using Diagnosis Related Groups (DRGs). 3M HIS Working Paper 5-98, Wallingford (3M HIS): 40 pp. (Online) http:// www.3m.com / us / healthcare / his / pdf / reports / evolcasemix5-98.pdf. (5 April 2013).

Averill, R., Goldfield, N., Steinbeck, B. & Grant, T. 1995. All Patient Refined Diagnosis Related Groups, 3M Health Information Systems, Wallingford, Connecticut.

Bahadori, K., Doyle-Waters, M.M., Marra, C., Lynd, L., Alasaly, K., Swiston, J. & Fitzgerald, J.M. 2009. Economic burden of asthma: a systematic review. *BMC Pulm Med* **9**:24. doi:10.1186/1471-2466-9-24.

Bailey, P.E. 1997. Costing pathology services: a practical approach to a difficult problem. *Pathology* **29**(2): 196-200.

Beck, E.J., Beecham, J., Mandalia, S., Griffith, R., Walters, M.D., Boulton, M. & Miller, D.L. 1999. What is the cost of getting the price wrong? *J Public Health Med* **21**(3):311-317.

Beecham, J. 1995. Collecting and estimating costs. In Knapp, M. (ed). The economic evaluation of mental health care. Arena. Ashgate Publishing Limited, London, UK. pp: 61-82.

Berlinguet, M., Vertrees, J., Freedman, R., Andrea, R. D. & Tinker, A. 2007. Case-mix Analysis Across Patient Populations and Boundaries: A Refined Classification System Designed Specifically for International Quality and Performance Use. 3M HIS.(Online)

|http://www.3m.com/ |Global Enterprise Digital Media Repository (14 April 2013).

Berman, P., Brotowasisto, Nadjib M., Sakai, S., & Gani, A. 1989. The costs of public primary health care services in rural Indonesia. *Bull World Health Organ* **67**(6):685-94.

Bigler, L. 2012. E-prescribing Benefits beyond Achieving Meaningful Use. *Drug Store News* **34** (8): 94.

Botz, C.K. 1989. Weighting Case Mix Groups: the Fatal Flaw in Resource Intensity Weights. *Health Management Forum***2**:8-11 http://hmf.sagepub.com/content/2/1/8.full.pdf.

Botz, C. K., Sutherland, J. & Lawrenson, J. 2006. Cost Weight Compression: Impact of Cost Data Precision and Completeness. *Health Care Financing Review*/spring **27** (3). (Online) http://www.cms.gov/Research-Statistics-Data-and-Systems/Research/HealthCare Financing Review/downloads/06Springpg111.pdf (31March 2013).

Bramkamp, M., Radovanovic, D., Erne, P.& Szucs, T.D. 2007. Determinants of costs and the length of stay in acute coronary syndromes: a real life analysis of more than 10,000 patients. *Cardiovasc Drugs Ther***21**(5):389-398. DOI 10.1007/s10557-007-6044-0.

Bridges, J, Haas, M. & Mazevska, D. 1999. A Qualitative Insight into Rural Case-mix Education. Case-mix Policy Unit, NSW Health Economics Training Program. CHERE Project Report 10. (Online) http://www.chere.uts.edu.au/pdf/r10.pdf (7 April 2013).

Brouwer, W., Rutten, F. & Koopmanschap, M. 2001. Costing in economic evaluations. In Drummond, M. & McGuire, A. (eds). Economic evaluation in health care. Merging theory with practice. Oxford University Press. pp: 68-93.

Busse, R., Geissler, A., Quentin, W. & Wiley, M. 2011. Diagnosis-Related Groups in Europe: Moving towards transparency, efficiency and quality in hospitals. Department of Health Care Management, Berlin University of Technology (WHO Collaborating Centre for Health Systems Research and Management) &European Observatory on Health Systems and Policies.

Canadian Institute for Health Information, 2012. Drivers of Prescription Drug Spending in Canada (Ottawa, Ont.: CIHI). (Online) http://www.cihi.ca/CIHI-ext-portal/pdf/internet/DRUG_SPEND_DRIVERS_EN (23 February 2015).

Carey, K. 2003.Hospital Length of Stay and Cost: A Multilevel Modeling Analysis. *Health Services and Outcomes Research Methodology* **3** (1): 41-56.

Centers for Medicare and Medicaid Services. 2011. National Health Expenditures Projections2011-2021. www.cms.gov/Research-Statistics-data-and-Systems/Statistics-Trends-and-Reports/NationalHealthExpendData/Downloads/Proj2011PDF.pdf.

Chilingerian, J. 2008. Origins of DRGs in the United States: A technical, political and cultural story, in J. Kimberly, G. de Pouvourville, T. D'Aunno, eds. *The Globalization of Managerial Innovation in Health Care*. Cambridge: Cambridge University Press.

Chow, W.L., Tin, A.S.& Meyyappan, A. 2010. Factors Influencing Costs of Inpatient Ischaemic Stroke Care in Singapore. *Proceedings of Singapore Healthcare* **19** (4):283-291.

Chua, H.T. & Cheah, J. 2012. Financing Universal Coverage in Malaysia: a case study. BMC Public Health **12**(Suppl 1): S1-S7.

Clinical casemix handbook, 2011-2012. Department of Health, Performance Activity and Quality Division, State of Western Australia 2011.) (Online) http://www.health.wa.gov.au/activity/docs/cch.pdf.(10 April 2013).

Cortoos, P-J., Gilissen, C., Laekeman, G., Peetermans, W.E., Leenaers, H., Vandorpe, L.& Simoens, S. 2013. Length of stay after reaching clinical stability drives hospital costs associated with adult community-acquired pneumonia. *Scandinavian journal of infectious disease* **45**(3): 219-226 (doi:10.3109/00365548.2012.726737).

Cotterill, P, Bobula, J & Connerton, R. 1986. Comparison of alternative relative weights for diagnosis-related groups. *Health Care Financ Rev* **7**(3): 37–51.

Coulsen, N.E. & Stuart, B.C. 1992. Persistence in the use of pharmaceuticals by the elderly: evidence from annual claims. *J Health Econ* **11**: 315–328.

Creese, A. & Parker, D. 1994. Cost analysis in primary health care: a training manual for programme managers. Geneva, WHO. Available at: http://whqlibdoc.who.int/publications/9241544708.pdf (20 April 2013).

Csomos, A., Janecsko, M. & Edbrooke, D. 2005. Comparative costing analysis of intensive care services between Hungary and United Kingdom. *Intensive CareMed*. Online publication by Springer. 2005 Jun 16.

Cyclus, J. & Irwin, R. 2010. The challenges of hospital payment systems. *Euro Observer – The Health Policy Bulletin of the European Observatory on Health Systems and Policies* **12**(3), (Online) http://www.euro.who.int/data/assets/pdf_file/0018/121743/euroObserver_ Autumn2010.pdf. (9 March 2013).

Dahlui, M., Wan, N.C. & Koon T.S. 2012. Cost analysis of UMMC services: estimating the unit cost for outpatient and inpatient services. *BMC Health Services Research* **12**(Suppl 1):O1.

Drummond, M., Manca, A. & Sculpher, M. 2005. Increasing the generalizability of economic evaluations: recommendations for the design, analysis, and reporting of studies. *Int J Technol Assess Health Care* **21**(2):165-71.

Duckett, S.J. 1998. Casemix funding for acute hospital inpatient services in Australia. eMJA**19**:s17–s21. https://www.mja.

com.au/journal/1998/169/8/casemix-funding-acute-hospital-inpatient-services-australia accessed 8/May/2014.

Edbrooke, D., Hibbert, C., Ridley, S., Long, T. & Dickie, H. 1999. The Intensive Care Working Group on Costing :The development of a method for comparative costing of individual intensive care units. *Anaesthesia* **54**(2):110-120.

Edwards, C., Metcalfe, D., Burn, A., Watson, K., Seward, F.C.N., Jephson, M.H. & van Zwanenberg, T.D. 1991.Influence of patient age on drug costs: an investigation to validate the prescribing unit. *International Journal of Pharmacy Practice***1**:73-8.

eHealth Initiative and Center for Improving Medication Management. 2008. *A Clinician's Guide to Electronic Prescribing.* (Online) http://www.aaos.org/research/committee/evidence/eprescribing-guide.pdf (23, February 2015).

Elliott, R. & Payne, K. 2005. Essentials of economic evaluation in healthcare. *Pharmaceutical Press*, London. pp: 45-63.

Evers, S.M., Struijs, J.N., Ament, A.J., van Genugten, M.L., Jager, J.H. & van den Bos, G.A. 2004. International comparison of stroke cost studies. *Stroke* **35**(5): 1209-1215.

Ezat, S.W.P., Syed, M.A. Mohd Rizal, A.M., Saperi, S., Ismail, S., Fuad, I & and Muhd, M.A. Azrif. 2013. Economic evaluation of monoclonal antibody in the management of colorectal cancer in Malaysia. *J Cancer Res Ther* **1**: 34–39. doi:10.14312/2052-4994.2013-5.

Falkenberg, T. & Tomson, G. 2000. The World Bank and Pharmaceuticals. *Health Policy & Planning* **15** (1): 52-58. (Online) http://heapol.oxfordjournals.org/content/15/1/52.long (29 March 2013).

Federal Register, 1995. **16** (106), pg. 29209.

Finkler SA. 1982. The distinction between cost and charges. *Ann Intern Med* **96** (1):102–109. http://dx.doi:10.7326/0003-4819-96-1-102 (23.December 2014).

Freeman, J., Fetter, R., Hayong, P., Schneider, K., Lichenstein, J., Hughes, J., Bauman, W., Duncan, C., Freeman, D. & Palmer, G. 1995. Diagnosis Related Group Refinement with Diagnosis- and Procedure- Specific Co morbidities and Complications. *Medical Care* **33**(8); 806-827.

Fetter, R.B. 1999. Casemix Classification System. *Australian Health Review* **22**(2): 1-23.

Fetter, R.B. 1993. Foreword, in M. Casas, M. Wiley, eds. *Diagnosis-Related Groups in Europe, Uses and Perspectives*. Berlin: Springer-Verlag.

Fetter, R.B., ed. 1991. *DRGs: Their Design and Development*. Ann Arbor, MI: Health Administration Press.

Fetter, R., Shin, Y., Freeman, J., Averill, R. & Thompson, J. 1980. Case mix definition by diagnosis-related groups. *Medical Care* **18** (2): 1-53.

Fischer, M.A., Vogeli, C., Stedman, M., Ferris, T., Brookhart, M.A. & Weissman, J.S. 2008.Effect of Electronic Prescribing With Formulary Decision Support on Medication Use and Cost. *Arch Intern Med* **168**(22):2433-2439. doi:10.1001/archinte.168.22.2433.

Fischer, W. 2000. A comparison of PCS construction principles of the American DRGs, the Austrian LDF system, and the German FP/S System. *Case-mix Quarterly* (21): 12-20. Available at: http://www.fischer-zim.ch/paper-en/PCS-Comparison-9909-PCSE.htm (3 March 2013).

Fischer, W. 1997. (Patient Classification Systems for Grouping Hospital Cases - Principles and Examples). BSV and Z/I/M, Bern and Wolfertswil 514 pp.

Gordon, S.&.C., Pockros, P.J., Terrault, N.A., Hoop, R.S., Buikema, A., Nerenz, D. Hamzeh, F.M. 2012. Impact of disease severity on healthcare costs in patients with chronic hepatitis C (CHC) virus infection. *Hepatology* **56** (5):1651–1660.

Gyldmark, M. 1995. A review of cost studies of intensive care units: problems with the cost concept. *Crit Care Med* **23**(5):964-72.

Hassali, M.A., Thambyappa, J., Nambiar, S., Shafie, A.A. & Löfgren, H. 2013. TRIPS, Free Trade Agreements and the Pharmaceutical Industry in Malaysia. In *"The New Political Economy of Pharmaceuticals: Production, Innnovation and TRIPS in the Global South"*, Eds Lofgren H and Williams OD. Palgrave Macmillan, Basingstoke, London, England, pp.152-166 pp 152-66.

Heavens, J. 1999. Case-mix – the missing link in South African healthcare management: an overview of case-mix groupings such as DRGs and HRGs, their use for improved clinical and administrative healthcare management, and recommendations for a way forward in South Africa. The Health Informatics R&D Co-ordination Programme of the Informatics & Communication Group, Medical Research Council, South Africa (online) http://www.mrc.ac.za/researchreports/casemix.pdf (7 February 013).

Heerey, A., McGowan, B., Ryan, M. & Barry, M. 2002. Microcosting versus DRGs in the provision of cost estimates for use in pharmacoeconomic evaluation.*Expert Rev Pharmacoecon Outcomes Res* **2** (1):29-33. Available at: http://informahealthcare.com/doi/abs/10.1586/14737167.2.1.29 (29 March 2013).

Hendriks, M.E., Kundu, P., Boers, A.C., Bolarinwa, O.A., Te Pas, M.J., Akande, T.M., Agbede, K., Gomez, G.B., Redekop, W.K., Schultsz, C. & Swan Tan, S. 2014. Step-by-step guideline for disease-specific costing studies in low- and middle-income countries: a mixed methodology. *Glob Health Action* 7:23573. http://dx.doi.org/10.3402/gha.v7.23573.

Heslop, L. 2012. Status of Costing Hospital Nursing Work within Australian Casemix Activity- Based Funding Policy. *International Journal of Nursing Practice.* **18**: 2-6.

Hoffman, J.M., Shah, N.D., Vermeulen, L.C., Schumock, G.T, Grim, P., Hunkler, R.J. & Hontz, K.H. 2006. Projecting future drug expenditures—2006. *Am J Health-Syst Pharm* **63**:123–138 (Online) (29 March 2013).

Hovenga, E.J.S. 1996. Casemix and information system, in health informatics: an overview, ed Hovenga, E., Kidd, M. & Cesnik, B., chapter 13, pp313-47 Churchill, Livingstone, Melbourne.

Jackson, T. 2001. Using computerized patient-level costing data for setting DRG weights: the Victorian (Australia) cost weight studies. *Health Policy* **56** (2):149-163. (Online) http://www.sciencedirect.com/science/article/pii/S0168851000001482# (31 March 2013).

James, C.V. 2005. The top down approach to allocate hospital costs and to computing relative weights. *MJPHM* **5**(Supplement 2): 75-90. (Online) http://www.mjphm.org.my/mjphm/journals/Volume%205%20%28Sup%202%29%20:%202005/Part%201.pdf (23 February 2013).

Jegers, M., Edbrooke, D.L., Hibbert, C.L., Chalfin, D.B. & Burchardi, H. 2002. Definitions and methods of cost assessment: an intensivist's guide. ESICM section on health research and outcome working group on cost effectiveness. *Intensive Care Med* **28**(6):680 – 685.

Kamaruddin MA. 2006. Universiti Kebangsaan Malaysia: historical background. Bangi: UKM Publisher.

Kaplan, W, & Mathers, C. 2011. The world medicine situation 2011: medicine expenditure; 2011. http://www.who.int/medicines/areas/policy/world_medicines_situation/en/.

Khan, N.A., Quan, H., Bugar, J.M., Lemaire, J.B., Brant, R. & Ghali, W.A. 2006. Association of postoperative complications with hospital costs and length of stay in a tertiary care center. *J Gen Intern Med* **21**:177-180.

Kobel, C., Thuilliez, J., Bellanger, M. & Pfeiffer, K-P. 2011. DRG systems and similar patient classification systems in Europe (chapter four, page 37 In Busse, R., Geissler, A., Quentin, W. & Wiley, M. (Eds.) Diagnosis Related Groups in Europe - Moving towards transparency, efficiency and quality in hospitals. (Online) http://www.euro.who.int/__data/assets/pdf_file/0004/162265/e96538.pdf (4 March 2013).

Ko, Y., Gwee, Y.S., Huang, Y.C., Chiang, J. & Chan, A. 2014. Costs and Length of Stay of Drug-Related Hospital Admissions in Cancer Patients. *Clinical therapeutics* **63**(4): 588–592. http://dx.doi.org/10.1016/j.clinthera.2014.02.014.

Langenbrunner, J., Cashin, C. & O'Dougherty S, editors. 2009. Designing and implementing health care provider payment systems: How to manuals. Washington DC: The World Bank; 2009. Available at: http://siteresources.worldbank.org/HEALTHNUTRITIONANDPOPULATION/Resources/Peer-Reviewed-Publications/ProviderPaymentHowTo.pdf (25 December 2014).

Lave, J., Pettengill, J., Schmid, L. & Vertrees, J. 1987. *Measurement issues in the development of a hospital case mix index for medicare.* Washington, D.C.: Congressional Research Service, The Library of Congress; 1987.

Lievens, Y., van den Bogaert, W. & Kesteloot, K. 2003. Activity-based costing: a practical model for cost calculation in radiotherapy. *Int J Radiat Oncol Biol Phys* **57**(2):522-35.

Lublóy, Á. 2014. Factors affecting the uptake of new medicines: a systematic literature review. *BMC Health Services Research* **14**:469 http://dx.doi:10.1186/1472-6963-14-469.

Luce, B.R., Manning, W.G., Siegel, J.E. & Lipscomb, J. 1996.Estimating costs in cost- effectiveness analysis. In *Cost effectiveness in health and medicine*; pp: 176-213. Edited by M.R. Gold, J.E. Siegel, L.B. Russell & M.C. Weinstein. New York: Oxford University Press.

Mathauer, I. & Wittenbecher, F. 2012. DRG-based payment systems in low- and middle-income countries: Implementation experiences and challenges. WHO, HSS/HSF/DP.E.10.2 (online) http://www.who.int/health_financing/documents/cov-dp_e_10_02-drg_systems/en/index.html (15 February 2013).

3M Health Information Systems. All Patient Refined DRG Software. 3MHealth Information Systems. (Online)://www.3mhis.com/product/apr_drg/brochure/menu.htm (17 April 2013).

Miller, R.A. & Gardner, R.M. 1997. Summary Recommendations for Responsible Monitoring and Regulation of Clinical Software Systems. Ann Intern Med 127:842–5.

Mills, A.J., Kapalamula, J. & Chisimbi, S. 1993. The cost of the district hospital: A case study in Malawi. *Bull World Health Organ* **71**:329-339.

Minh, H.V., Giang, K.B., Huong, D.L., Huong, le. T., Huong, N.T., Giang, P.N., Hoat, L.N.& Wright, P. 2009. Costing of clinical services in rural district hospitals in northern Vietnam. *Int J Health Plann Manage* **25**(1):63–73.

Miranda, M. & Cortez, L. 2005. The Diagnosis Related Group (DRGs) to adjust payment-mechanism for health system providers. Inter-American conference on social security, México, D.F. CISS/WP/05122. (Online) http://www.ciss.org.mx/pdf/en/studies/CISS-WP-05122.pdf (17 February 2013).

Mogyorosy, Z. & Smith, P. 2005. *The main methodological issues in costing health care services:* a literature review. Centre for Health Economics, University of York. Available at: http://www.york.ac.uk/media/che/documents/papers/researchpapers/rp7_Methodological_issues_in_costing_health_care_services.pdf (19 March 2013).

Mohd Ali Kamaruddin. 2006. Universiti Kebangsaan Malaysia: Sejarah Penubuhan. Penerbit Universiti Kebangsaan Malaysia, Bangi.

Muennig, P. & Kahn, K. 2002. Designing and conducting cost-effectiveness analysis in medicine and health care. Jossey-Bass. A Wiley Company. pp: 134- 157.

Mullin, R.L., Hughes, J. & Averill, R.F. 2003. International Refined Diagnosis Related Groups, Version 2.0. 306. 11-10-2003. Washington, DC. *Proceedings of the 19th International Case Mix Conference.* 11-10-2003.

Mullin, R.L., Vertrees, J.C., Freeman, R., Castioni, R., & Tinker, A. 2002. Case-mix analysis across patient populations and boundaries: a refined classification system designed specifically for international use.(online)|http://www.3m.com/ (16 February 2013).

Munoz E, Josephson J, Tenenbaum N, Goldstein J, Shears AM, Wise L. 1989. Diagnosis-related groups, costs, and outcome for patients in the intensive care unit. *Heart Lung* **18**:627– 633.

Nathan, H., Atoria, C.L., Bach, P.B. & Elkin, E.B. 2014. Hospital Volume, Complications, and Cost of Cancer Surgery in the Elderly. *JCO JCO***57**:7155;

Narong, D.K. 2009. Activity-based costing and management solutions to traditional shortcomings of cost accounting. *Cost Engineering*, **51**(8):11-18.

Negrini, D., Kettle, A., Sheppard, L., Mills, G.H. & Edbrooke, D.L. 2004. The cost of a hospital ward in Europe: is there a methodology available to accurately measure the costs? *J Health Organ Manag* **18**(2-3):195-206.

Newhouse, J.P., Cretin, S & Witsberger, C.J.1989.Predicting hospital accounting costs. *Health Care Financ Rev* **11**(1): 25–33.

Nikkel, L.E., Fox, E.J., Black, K.P., Davis, C., Andersen, L. & Hollenbeak, C.S. 2012. Impact of comorbidities on hospitalization costs following hip fracture. *J Bone Joint Surg Am* **94**(1):9-17. doi: 10.2106/JBJS.J.01077.

Nor Azlin, M.N., Aljunid, S.M.A., Aziz, N.A., Amrizal, M.N. & Sulong, S. 2012. Direct medical cost of stroke: findings from a tertiary hospital in Malaysia. *Med J Mal* **675**(5):468–472.

OECD. 2011. Pharmaceutical expenditure, in *Health at a Glance2011: OECD Indicators*, OECD Publishing. (Online) http://dx.doi.org/10.1787/health_glance-2011-63-en (29 March 2013).

Orlewska, E. & Mierzejewski, P. 2003. Guidelines for cost calculation in economic evaluations of healthcare programs. *Farmakoekonomika* [Poland] 1. Online edition. http://www.czytelniamedyczna.pl/424, guidelines-for-cost-calculation-in-economic-evaluations-of-healthcare-programs-p.html.

Palmer, G., Aisbett, C., Milis, N., Xu, C. 1998. The integration of the clinical and cost modeling approaches to case-mix costing. *Case-mix Quarterly* **0** (1):1-10.

Palmer, G. & Hindle, D. 2000. Introduction to case-mix for master student s. Session 1, 2000. School of Health Services Management, (revised by Tessa Ho). HEAL 9743, the University of New South Wales, Australia.

Park, M., Braun, T., Carrin, G. & Evans, D.B. 2007. Provider payments and cost containment lessons from OECD countries. Technical briefs for policy makers. Department of health system financing and health financing policy, Geneva, WHO/HSS/HSF/PB/07.02. Available at: http://hdl.handle.net/10067/673070151162165141 (7 March 2013).

Petitti, D.B. 2000. Meta-analysis, decision analysis and cost-effectiveness analysis. Methods for quantitative synthesis in medicine. Second Edition. Oxford University Press. pp: 190-2001.

Peiró, S., Gómez, G., Navarro, M., Guadarrama, I. & Rejas, J. 2004. On behalf of the Psychosp Group: Length of stay and antipsychotic treatment costs of patients with acute psychosis admitted to hospital in Spain. Description and associated factors. *The Psychosp study Soc Psychiatry Psychiatr Epidemiol* **39**: 507– 13.

Riewpaiboon, A., Jaroenkitpan, N. & Wipaswacharayotin, Y. 2005. Cost structure of hospital-based pharmaceutical services: a consideration of reimbursement. *Mahidol Univ J Pharm Sci* **32**:47–54.

Roberts, S.J. & Harris, C.M. 1993. Age, sex, and temporary resident originated prescribing units (ASTRO-PUs): new weightings for analysing prescribing of general practices in England. *BMJ* **307**(6902): 485–488.

Rodrigues, J.M. 1993. DRGs: origin and dissemination throughout Europe, in M. Casas, M. Wiley, eds. Diagnosis-Related Groups in Europe, Uses and Perspectives. Berlin: Springer-Verlag.

Rohaizat, Y. 2005. Proposed national health care financing mechanism for Malaysia: the role of case-mix. *Malaysian Journal of Public Health Medicine* **5**(2). (online) http://www.mjphm.org.my/mjphm/journals/Volume%205%20%28Sup%202%29%20:%202005/Part%201.pdf (28 February 2013).

Rohaizat, Y., Amrizl, M. N., Saperi, S. & Aljunid. S. 2005. Cost analysis and cost weight for the treatment of orthopedic cases in a teaching hospital in malaysia using the case-mix approach: the experience of UKM hospital, *Malaysian Journal Of Public Health Medicine* 5 (supplement 2): 63-73. Available at: http://www.mjphm.org.my/mjphm/journals/Volume%205%20%28Sup%202%29%20:%202005/Part%201.pdf (25 February 2013).

Rosenthal, E. 2014. *Officials Question the Rising Costs of Generic Drugs*. The New York Times. 7 October 2014. (Online) http://www.nytimes.com/2014/10/08/business/officials-question-the-rising-costs-of-generic-drugs.html?_r=1 (30 January 2015).

Rogowski, J.R. & Byrne, D.J. 1990. Comparison of alternative weight recalibration methods for diagnosis-related groups. *Health Care Financing Review* 12 (2): 87–101.

Saperi, B.S., Amrizal, M.N., Rohaizat, B.Y., Zafar, A., & Syed Aljunid. 2005. Implementation of case-mix in hospital UKM: the progress. *Malaysian Journal of Public Health Medicine* 5 (2): 45 – 53. http://www.mjphm.org.my/mjphm/journals/Volume%205%20%28Sup%202%29%20:%202005/Part%201.pdf (20 February 2013).

Siddiqui, M. & Rajkumar, S.V. 2012. The High Cost of Cancer Drugs and What We Can Do About It. *Mayo Clin Proc* 87(10): 935–943.

Shepard, D.S., Hodgkin, D. & Anthony, Y.E. 2000. Analysis of hospital costs: a manual for managers. Geneva: World Health Organization; 2000.

Street, A. & Dawson, D. 2002. Costing hospital activity: the experience with healthcare resource groups in England. *Eur J Health Econ* 3(1): 3-9.

Suhil, M.A., Hassali, M.A.A, & Ibrahim, M. 2010. Evaluation of direct medical cost in treating hypertension in a Malaysian public university. *AJPCR* 3 (3): 170-173.

Teich, J.M., Osheroff, J.A., Pifer EA, Sittig, D.F., Jenders, R.A. :CDS Expert Review Panel. 2005.Clinical decision support in electronic prescribing; Recommendations and an action plan. *J AM Med Inform Assoc* **12**:365-376.

Thomas, C. P., M. Kim, A. McDonald, P. Kreiner, S. J. Kelleher, M. B. Blackman, Kaufman, P.N. & Carrow, G.M. 2012. Prescribers' Expectations and Barriers to Electronic Prescribing of Controlled Substances. *Journal of the American Medical Informatics Association* **19**(3): 375–81.

Tsilaajav, T. 2009. *Costing study for selected hospitals in the Philippines*, Technical Assistance to the Health Sector Policy Programme in the Philippines an EC-GOP joint Programme implemented by the DoH and F1 provinces.(on line) http://www.doh.gov.ph/sites/default/files/Costing%20Study%20for%20Selected%20Hospitals%20in%20the%20Philippines.pdf (April 2013).

Thompson, J.D., Averill, R.F. & Fetter, R.B. 1979. Planning, Budgeting, and Controlling – One Look at the Future: Casemix Cost Accounting. *Health Services Research* **14**, 111-125.

UKMMC 2002. *Sistem Case-Mix Hospital Universiti Kebangsaan Malaysia*. Malaysia: Universiti Kebangsaan Malaysia.

Universiti Kebangsaan Malaysia (UKM-Website). 2013. (Online) http://transformasi.ukm.my/index.php/en/home/history. (5 February 2013).

Vander Plaetse B., Hlatiwayo, G., Van Eygen, L., Meessen, B. & Criel, B. 2005. Costs and revenue of health care in a rural Zimbabwean district. Health Policy Plan20(4):243-251.

Van Vliet, R.C.J.A. 1992. Predictability of individual health care expenditures. *J Risk Insur.* 1992;**59**:443– 460.

Vaughan-Sarrazin, M., Bayman, L., Rasenthal, G., Herderson, W., Hendricks, A. & Cullen, J.J. 2011. The business case for the reduction of surgical complications in VA hospitals. *Surgery* **149**:474-483.

Wagner DP, Wineland TD, Knaus WA. 1983. The hidden costs of treating severely ill patients: charges and resource consumption in an intensive care unit. *Health Care Financing* Rev **5**:81– 86.

Wang, X.J., Wong, M., Hsu, L.Y. & Chan, A. 2014. Costs associated with febrile neutropenia in solid tumor and lymphoma patients - an observational study in Singapore. *BMC Health Serv Res* **14**:434. doi: 10.1186/1472-6963-14-434.

Waters, H. & Hussey, P. 2004. Pricing health services for purchasers: a review of methods and experiences. HNP Discussion Paper. World Bank, Washington, USA.

West, T.D., Balas, E.A.& West, D.A. 1996. Contrasting RCC, RVU, and ABC for managed care decisions. A case study compares three widely used costing methods and finds one superior. *Healthc Financ Manage* **50**(8):54-61.

WHO. 2004. The World Medicines Situation. 2004. Chapter 5 & Annex 2. WHO/EDM/PAR/2004. Available at: http://apps.who.int/medicinedocs/en/d/Js6160e/2.html#Js6160e.2 / (29 March 2013).

Wouters, A.V. 1991.Disaggregated annual health care expenditures: their predictability and role as predictors. *Health Serv Res* **26**:247–272.

Wrobel, M.V., Doshi, J., Stuart, B.C. & Briesacher B. 2003. Predictability of prescription drug expenditures for Medicare beneficiaries. *Health Care Financ Rev* **25**: 37– 46.

Ye Lu, Hernandez, P., Abegunde, D. & Edejer, T. 2011. The world medicine situation 2011: medicine expenditure. WHO/EMP/MIE/2011.2.6 (Online) http://apps.who.int/medicinedocs/documents/s18767en/s18767en.pdf (29March 2013).

Zhao, Y., Ash, A.S., Ellis, R.P., Ayanian, J.Z., Pope, G.C., Bowen, B. & Weyuker, L. 2005. Predicting pharmacy costs and other medical costs using diagnoses and drug claims. Med Care 43(1):34-43.

Zimmerman, J.L. 2003. Accounting for decision-making and control. International edition. Fourth edition. McGraw-Hill Irwin. Boston. pp: 29-75.

Zoucas, E. & Lydrup, M-L. 2014. Hospital costs associated with surgical morbidity after elective colorectal procedures: a retrospective observational cohort study in 530 patients. *Patient Safety in Surgery* **8**:2.

APPENDIX

APPENDIX A

PHARMACY SERVICE WEIGHTS OF 450 UTILIZED MY-DRGS

MY-DRG	No. of Episodes Per DRG	Total Pharmacy Cost per DRG	Average Pharmacy Cost per DRG	Pharmacy Service Weight
C-4-11-III	38	204588.16	5383.90	11.0762
B-1-10-III	11	49817.84	4528.89	9.3172
J-1-20-III	5	22178.34	4435.67	9.1254
U-1-20-III	17	61664.92	3627.35	7.4625
M-1-20-III	5	16848.74	3369.75	6.9325
C-4-10-III	31	104232.86	3362.35	6.9173
G-1-11-III	14	46170.40	3297.89	6.7847
M-1-60-III	8	22978.67	2872.33	5.9092
S-4-13-III	6	17148.36	2858.06	5.8798
D-4-10-III	13	34282.24	2637.10	5.4252
B-1-11-III	7	18080.84	2582.98	5.3139
M-1-03-III	11	26994.90	2454.08	5.0487
J-4-12-III	9	20444.37	2271.60	4.6733
G-4-21-III	5	10925.50	2185.10	4.4954
D-1-10-I	9	18569.22	2063.25	4.2447
I-4-13-III	6	11693.31	1948.89	4.0094
I-1-04-III	5	9550.77	1910.15	3.9297
D-1-20-III	5	9455.59	1891.12	3.8905
K-1-20-III	16	30134.09	1883.38	3.8746
I-4-14-III	10	18375.21	1837.52	3.7803
J-1-30-III	13	23578.18	1813.71	3.7313
A-4-10-III	75	134026.95	1787.03	3.6764
K-1-40-III	18	31168.62	1731.59	3.5624
B-4-11-III	12	20474.17	1706.18	3.5101
B-1-13-III	6	10220.75	1703.46	3.5045
N-1-20-III	11	18300.29	1663.66	3.4226
G-4-18-II	9	14547.33	1616.37	3.3253
G-4-19-III	10	16137.12	1613.71	3.3198
G-1-10-III	19	29990.75	1578.46	3.2473
M-1-02-III	16	23884.79	1492.80	3.0711
B-1-10-II	9	13127.25	1458.58	3.0007
B-4-13-III	19	27385.56	1441.35	2.9652

MY-DRG	No. of Episodes Per DRG	Total Pharmacy Cost per DRG	Average Pharmacy Cost per DRG	Pharmacy Service Weight
K-1-30-III	5	6935.28	1387.06	2.8536
C-4-11-I	6	8236.42	1372.74	2.8241
L-4-11-III	23	31437.28	1366.84	2.8120
A-4-14-III	11	14119.63	1283.60	2.6407
M-4-21-III	12	15354.77	1279.56	2.6324
L-1-30-III	10	12522.15	1252.22	2.5762
I-1-20-III	28	34609.91	1236.07	2.5429
I-1-07-III	9	10900.83	1211.20	2.4918
C-4-11-II	33	39699.00	1203.00	2.4749
L-1-40-III	18	21252.01	1180.67	2.4290
M-1-02-II	15	17406.58	1160.44	2.3873
M-1-70-III	11	12648.29	1149.84	2.3655
L-1-20-I	6	6593.53	1098.92	2.2608
M-4-16-III	12	12887.18	1073.93	2.2094
M-4-17-III	12	12732.36	1061.03	2.1828
G-4-11-III	12	12533.28	1044.44	2.1487
G-1-11-II	12	12329.91	1027.49	2.1138
N-1-12-III	8	8192.59	1024.07	2.1068
J-4-15-III	52	52995.82	1019.15	2.0967
I-4-23-III	12	12224.06	1018.67	2.0957
K-4-12-II	18	18246.98	1013.72	2.0855
K-4-12-III	6	6069.53	1011.59	2.0811
W-4-10-III	18	18099.79	1005.54	2.0687
C-4-14-III	15	14888.41	992.56	2.0420
U-4-10-III	16	15795.33	987.21	2.0310
M-1-30-III	8	7865.23	983.15	2.0226
B-1-10-I	18	17670.83	981.71	2.0197
J-4-21-III	43	41346.12	961.54	1.9781
N-4-12-III	34	32616.94	959.32	1.9736
M-4-19-II	8	7661.98	957.75	1.9703
M-4-13-III	11	10348.76	940.80	1.9355
C-4-10-II	35	32441.72	926.91	1.9069

MY-DRG	No. of Episodes Per DRG	Total Pharmacy Cost per DRG	Average Pharmacy Cost per DRG	Pharmacy Service Weight
V-4-10-III	9	8277.90	919.77	1.8922
Z-4-12-III	17	15451.39	908.91	1.8699
B-1-13-II	5	4543.14	908.63	1.8693
A-4-10-II	40	36315.66	907.89	1.8678
L-1-30-II	17	15424.15	907.30	1.8666
I-1-07-II	7	6229.60	889.94	1.8309
N-4-11-III	13	11535.13	887.32	1.8255
A-4-11-II	13	11455.83	881.22	1.8129
M-4-15-II	5	4375.58	875.12	1.8004
A-4-14-II	18	15266.42	848.13	1.7448
M-4-19-III	5	4222.43	844.49	1.7373
M-4-10-III	19	16043.93	844.42	1.7372
K-1-20-II	22	18259.87	829.99	1.7075
M-4-10-II	20	15713.40	785.67	1.6163
B-4-14-III	18	13812.41	767.36	1.5787
S-4-13-II	16	12151.22	759.45	1.5624
J-4-17-III	74	55015.41	743.45	1.5295
E-4-13-III	11	8134.39	739.49	1.5213
J-4-15-I	12	8733.88	727.82	1.4973
N-1-20-II	16	11626.71	726.67	1.4950
G-4-18-III	9	6522.42	724.71	1.4909
A-4-11-III	7	5048.91	721.27	1.4839
K-1-30-II	14	10054.71	718.19	1.4775
B-4-13-II	20	14322.52	716.13	1.4733
M-1-40-II	13	9285.06	714.24	1.4694
G-4-17-II	11	7691.53	699.23	1.4385
J-4-20-III	14	9778.63	698.47	1.4370
V-4-10-II	15	10459.55	697.30	1.4345
J-4-16-III	75	52259.64	696.80	1.4335
L-4-14-III	11	7589.00	689.91	1.4193
I-4-24-III	10	6854.55	685.46	1.4102
N-4-12-II	30	20540.22	684.67	1.4086

MY-DRG	No. of Episodes Per DRG	Total Pharmacy Cost per DRG	Average Pharmacy Cost per DRG	Pharmacy Service Weight
M-1-20-II	20	13489.62	674.48	1.3876
K-1-50-III	5	3244.35	648.87	1.3349
G-1-10-II	17	11009.24	647.60	1.3323
H-1-20-II	13	8414.16	647.24	1.3316
J-4-21-II	35	22324.31	637.84	1.3122
I-4-10-III	25	15917.02	636.68	1.3098
L-4-10-III	17	10819.40	636.44	1.3093
I-1-07-I	6	3810.25	635.04	1.3065
N-4-10-III	42	25960.14	618.10	1.2716
G-4-22-III	23	14215.33	618.06	1.2715
G-4-11-I	7	4321.53	617.36	1.2701
M-4-16-I	15	9222.50	614.83	1.2649
L-4-12-III	33	20253.16	613.73	1.2626
B-4-11-II	30	18094.18	603.14	1.2408
J-4-17-I	43	25721.05	598.16	1.2306
B-1-12-I	10	5936.07	593.61	1.2212
G-4-26-III	19	11238.24	591.49	1.2168
D-4-13-III	19	11217.79	590.41	1.2146
G-4-11-II	20	11782.53	589.13	1.2120
J-4-14-III	35	20289.90	579.71	1.1926
K-4-18-III	41	23575.96	575.02	1.1830
M-4-16-II	30	17110.35	570.35	1.1734
J-4-16-II	75	42327.36	564.36	1.1611
J-4-15-II	27	15227.38	563.98	1.1603
V-1-14-III	5	2815.24	563.05	1.1583
N-4-13-III	10	5610.24	561.02	1.1542
E-4-10-III	27	14917.00	552.48	1.1366
I-4-12-III	91	49996.16	549.41	1.1303
J-4-17-II	73	40060.74	548.78	1.1290
I-4-13-II	7	3772.65	538.95	1.1088
M-1-80-III	7	3716.78	530.97	1.0923
I-1-40-III	14	7218.33	515.60	1.0607

MY-DRG	No. of Episodes Per DRG	Total Pharmacy Cost per DRG	Average Pharmacy Cost per DRG	Pharmacy Service Weight
S-4-12-III	12	6183.74	515.31	1.0601
J-1-30-II	9	4637.06	515.23	1.0600
B-4-11-I	8	4118.87	514.86	1.0592
L-4-10-II	13	6680.21	513.86	1.0572
N-1-40-III	6	3065.78	510.96	1.0512
K-4-15-III	9	4546.85	505.21	1.0393
M-4-14-II	6	3010.88	501.81	1.0324
K-4-10-III	21	10504.34	500.21	1.0291
F-4-16-III	15	7291.24	486.08	1.0000
H-4-10-I	7	3358.30	479.76	0.9870
I-4-16-III	16	7660.48	478.78	0.9850
G-4-14-III	22	10485.51	476.61	0.9805
M-1-04-II	15	7131.73	475.45	0.9781
K-4-13-I	18	8474.54	470.81	0.9686
V-4-11-III	11	4792.17	435.65	0.8963
I-4-19-III	23	9981.74	433.99	0.8928
M-1-20-I	19	7985.95	420.31	0.8647
M-1-02-I	13	5443.11	418.70	0.8614
V-1-13-II	11	4545.85	413.26	0.8502
G-4-24-III	13	5335.69	410.44	0.8444
I-1-15-III	30	12264.24	408.81	0.8410
B-4-14-II	22	8938.92	406.31	0.8359
J-4-18-III	41	16377.73	399.46	0.8218
K-4-16-II	11	4389.10	399.01	0.8209
N-4-11-I	18	7032.31	390.68	0.8037
I-4-23-II	24	9366.86	390.29	0.8029
V-4-11-II	5	1932.83	386.57	0.7953
I-4-15-III	23	8867.70	385.55	0.7932
J-4-18-II	59	22510.91	381.54	0.7849
B-1-11-II	5	1906.43	381.29	0.7844
G-1-30-II	9	3419.76	379.97	0.7817
N-4-11-II	18	6827.01	379.28	0.7803

MY-DRG	No. of Episodes Per DRG	Total Pharmacy Cost per DRG	Average Pharmacy Cost per DRG	Pharmacy Service Weight
N-1-40-II	11	4168.06	378.91	0.7795
K-4-18-II	53	19778.89	373.19	0.7677
M-1-70-II	16	5959.20	372.45	0.7662
J-4-20-II	19	6949.01	365.74	0.7524
G-4-13-III	6	2172.44	362.07	0.7449
E-4-11-III	43	15057.15	350.17	0.7204
I-4-12-II	76	26490.85	348.56	0.7171
E-4-13-II	13	4512.35	347.10	0.7141
M-4-10-I	16	5516.61	344.79	0.7093
V-1-14-II	15	5131.67	342.11	0.7038
E-1-20-II	14	4779.97	341.43	0.7024
M-1-03-II	20	6811.35	340.57	0.7006
M-4-12-III	7	2367.80	338.26	0.6959
M-4-18-III	7	2350.53	335.79	0.6908
K-1-20-I	52	17394.11	334.50	0.6882
C-4-10-I	20	6576.23	328.81	0.6765
I-4-10-II	32	10512.67	328.52	0.6759
H-4-12-II	16	5212.55	325.78	0.6702
K-1-40-II	24	7728.42	322.02	0.6625
G-1-10-I	25	8030.00	321.20	0.6608
K-4-11-III	16	5097.18	318.57	0.6554
A-4-13-III	16	5096.05	318.50	0.6552
K-1-30-I	11	3481.35	316.49	0.6511
M-4-20-II	7	2208.80	315.54	0.6492
U-4-10-I	19	5915.49	311.34	0.6405
U-4-15-II	18	5603.83	311.32	0.6405
H-4-12-III	6	1864.58	310.76	0.6393
L-1-40-II	21	6524.39	310.69	0.6392
I-1-30-II	10	3101.42	310.14	0.6380
I-1-20-II	34	10421.26	306.51	0.6306
K-1-10-II	6	1827.08	304.51	0.6265
M-1-30-II	20	6072.94	303.65	0.6247

MY-DRG	No. of Episodes Per DRG	Total Pharmacy Cost per DRG	Average Pharmacy Cost per DRG	Pharmacy Service Weight
M-4-21-II	23	6952.80	302.30	0.6219
G-4-19-I	8	2414.62	301.83	0.6209
I-4-20-III	59	17510.90	296.79	0.6106
A-4-11-I	13	3834.48	294.96	0.6068
G-4-15-II	20	5871.24	293.56	0.6039
I-4-19-II	37	10849.32	293.22	0.6032
G-4-22-II	41	11985.42	292.33	0.6014
M-4-19-I	13	3749.22	288.40	0.5933
W-1-01-I	16	4602.13	287.63	0.5917
J-4-14-I	10	2855.20	285.52	0.5874
U-1-20-II	13	3663.39	281.80	0.5797
L-4-11-II	37	10295.70	278.26	0.5725
K-1-12-II	6	1654.06	275.68	0.5671
K-4-15-II	13	3540.55	272.35	0.5603
M-1-60-II	15	4081.22	272.08	0.5597
I-4-20-II	123	33036.48	268.59	0.5526
F-4-13-III	6	1603.11	267.19	0.5497
I-4-10-I	33	8808.33	266.92	0.5491
F-4-11-II	13	3449.79	265.37	0.5459
B-1-14-II	20	5300.70	265.04	0.5452
I-4-20-I	150	39473.27	263.16	0.5414
L-4-12-II	39	10255.46	262.96	0.5410
A-4-12-III	8	2100.94	262.62	0.5403
M-4-13-II	19	4983.83	262.31	0.5396
N-1-30-II	11	2872.16	261.11	0.5372
S-4-13-I	18	4657.54	258.75	0.5323
M-1-03-I	40	10343.64	258.59	0.5320
I-4-15-II	26	6615.25	254.43	0.5234
G-4-10-I	5	1263.02	252.60	0.5197
M-1-04-I	36	9038.03	251.06	0.5165
K-4-11-II	34	8411.35	247.39	0.5090
U-1-15-II	5	1234.20	246.84	0.5078

MY-DRG	No. of Episodes Per DRG	Total Pharmacy Cost per DRG	Average Pharmacy Cost per DRG	Pharmacy Service Weight
C-4-14-II	8	1968.84	246.11	0.5063
G-4-13-II	18	4407.58	244.87	0.5038
F-4-13-II	7	1698.57	242.65	0.4992
M-1-80-II	19	4603.31	242.28	0.4984
M-1-70-I	31	7499.29	241.91	0.4977
I-1-20-I	16	3827.16	239.20	0.4921
E-4-11-II	50	11905.93	238.12	0.4899
I-4-17-III	12	2853.81	237.82	0.4893
F-4-16-I	12	2848.70	237.39	0.4884
N-4-16-III	16	3736.95	233.56	0.4805
G-1-30-I	8	1845.72	230.72	0.4746
I-1-15-II	50	11492.11	229.84	0.4728
S-4-12-II	14	3163.07	225.93	0.4648
V-1-13-III	7	1577.96	225.42	0.4638
L-4-10-I	18	3947.02	219.28	0.4511
V-4-10-I	5	1094.06	218.81	0.4502
L-4-11-I	16	3490.57	218.16	0.4488
C-4-14-I	16	3478.36	217.40	0.4472
I-4-24-I	18	3909.18	217.18	0.4468
M-4-18-II	13	2778.77	213.75	0.4397
L-1-30-I	17	3623.23	213.13	0.4385
I-4-16-II	9	1899.72	211.08	0.4342
J-4-14-II	29	6091.70	210.06	0.4321
F-4-10-II	14	2936.33	209.74	0.4315
D-4-13-II	40	8271.28	206.78	0.4254
I-4-24-II	15	3095.86	206.39	0.4246
J-4-16-I	87	17595.84	202.25	0.4161
H-4-11-I	7	1399.48	199.93	0.4113
W-4-10-II	64	12711.52	198.62	0.4086
E-4-10-II	40	7934.24	198.36	0.4081
K-1-11-I	5	971.87	194.37	0.3999
U-1-10-I	5	971.38	194.28	0.3997

MY-DRG	No. of Episodes Per DRG	Total Pharmacy Cost per DRG	Average Pharmacy Cost per DRG	Pharmacy Service Weight
B-1-11-I	9	1740.89	193.43	0.3979
U-1-12-II	6	1158.76	193.13	0.3973
I-1-40-II	16	3063.92	191.50	0.3940
G-4-14-I	9	1716.02	190.67	0.3923
F-4-10-I	117	22217.33	189.89	0.3907
K-4-16-I	5	945.96	189.19	0.3892
G-4-14-II	39	7176.39	184.01	0.3786
Z-4-12-I	17	3107.01	182.77	0.3760
W-1-20-II	23	4198.07	182.52	0.3755
I-4-15-I	36	6528.57	181.35	0.3731
N-4-10-I	41	7420.47	180.99	0.3723
G-4-17-I	13	2297.03	176.69	0.3635
K-4-10-II	52	9185.68	176.65	0.3634
N-1-20-I	22	3872.10	176.00	0.3621
I-1-15-I	73	12800.07	175.34	0.3607
I-4-16-I	15	2629.24	175.28	0.3606
N-4-10-II	132	23043.04	174.57	0.3591
I-4-18-II	5	864.21	172.84	0.3556
K-1-50-II	9	1549.77	172.20	0.3543
J-1-30-I	15	2570.21	171.35	0.3525
G-1-11-I	9	1536.59	170.73	0.3512
I-4-17-II	14	2378.18	169.87	0.3495
J-4-18-I	83	14070.72	169.53	0.3488
H-1-30-II	34	5753.05	169.21	0.3481
K-4-13-II	15	2536.31	169.09	0.3479
M-4-17-II	35	5903.55	168.67	0.3470
M-4-13-I	14	2339.93	167.14	0.3438
S-4-12-I	18	2993.87	166.33	0.3422
E-4-10-I	37	6114.44	165.26	0.3400
G-4-24-II	17	2780.89	163.58	0.3365
F-4-13-I	72	11625.96	161.47	0.3322
L-4-14-II	10	1603.65	160.37	0.3299

MY-DRG	No. of Episodes Per DRG	Total Pharmacy Cost per DRG	Average Pharmacy Cost per DRG	Pharmacy Service Weight
U-4-13-III	20	3204.85	160.24	0.3297
O-6-10-III	12	1900.49	158.37	0.3258
W-4-16-III	19	3007.99	158.32	0.3257
K-4-15-I	17	2687.63	158.10	0.3252
H-4-11-II	6	936.45	156.08	0.3211
G-4-15-III	18	2805.00	155.83	0.3206
M-1-30-I	22	3425.15	155.69	0.3203
K-4-17-III	31	4788.82	154.48	0.3178
N-4-12-I	22	3390.17	154.10	0.3170
W-4-10-I	13	1985.66	152.74	0.3142
F-4-11-I	62	9428.10	152.07	0.3128
K-1-13-II	16	2383.55	148.97	0.3065
S-4-16-I	14	2075.88	148.28	0.3050
D-4-11-II	7	1030.03	147.15	0.3027
K-4-11-I	24	3522.32	146.76	0.3019
G-4-16-III	13	1893.75	145.67	0.2997
G-4-10-II	5	720.90	144.18	0.2966
U-4-10-II	72	10263.70	142.55	0.2933
I-1-40-I	28	3955.80	141.28	0.2906
D-4-14-I	15	2095.90	139.73	0.2875
K-4-10-I	37	5132.00	138.70	0.2853
H-4-12-I	50	6883.34	137.67	0.2832
M-4-18-I	18	2440.02	135.56	0.2789
L-4-12-I	80	10831.68	135.40	0.2785
B-4-14-I	44	5943.04	135.07	0.2779
Z-4-12-II	13	1754.74	134.98	0.2777
F-4-15-I	12	1617.10	134.76	0.2772
I-4-13-I	7	942.85	134.69	0.2771
M-1-40-I	24	3203.41	133.48	0.2746
V-1-14-I	19	2530.61	133.19	0.2740
G-4-26-II	22	2826.89	128.50	0.2643
J-4-21-I	22	2812.58	127.84	0.2630

MY-DRG	No. of Episodes Per DRG	Total Pharmacy Cost per DRG	Average Pharmacy Cost per DRG	Pharmacy Service Weight
I-1-17-I	11	1403.21	127.56	0.2624
M-1-50-I	30	3809.38	126.98	0.2612
F-4-16-II	8	1014.82	126.85	0.2610
G-4-15-I	8	1010.03	126.25	0.2597
N-4-16-II	32	3969.48	124.05	0.2552
J-1-20-II	5	619.81	123.96	0.2550
O-6-10-II	113	13810.18	122.21	0.2514
D-4-14-II	7	852.31	121.76	0.2505
W-4-12-I	23	2797.36	121.62	0.2502
U-1-12-I	10	1193.19	119.32	0.2455
A-4-14-I	9	1030.43	114.49	0.2355
M-1-60-I	77	8803.58	114.33	0.2352
K-4-12-I	15	1711.10	114.07	0.2347
L-4-13-II	14	1566.06	111.86	0.2301
E-4-13-I	27	2994.80	110.92	0.2282
K-1-10-I	11	1208.60	109.87	0.2260
M-4-14-I	7	765.67	109.38	0.2250
K-1-40-I	68	7436.94	109.37	0.2250
U-1-11-I	23	2498.87	108.65	0.2235
L-1-50-I	55	5970.72	108.56	0.2233
M-1-80-I	86	9317.89	108.35	0.2229
M-4-17-I	115	12458.32	108.33	0.2229
U-1-20-I	61	6603.03	108.25	0.2227
W-1-30-II	35	3755.59	107.30	0.2208
I-4-12-I	20	2126.72	106.34	0.2188
O-6-11-I	7	742.54	106.08	0.2182
V-1-12-II	5	525.68	105.14	0.2163
N-1-40-I	51	5357.68	105.05	0.2161
B-4-13-I	19	1992.96	104.89	0.2158
L-1-40-I	66	6867.05	104.05	0.2141
O-6-12-III	17	1764.93	103.82	0.2136
O-6-13-III	20	2075.30	103.77	0.2135

MY-DRG	No. of Episodes Per DRG	Total Pharmacy Cost per DRG	Average Pharmacy Cost per DRG	Pharmacy Service Weight
I-4-18-I	16	1653.54	103.35	0.2126
K-4-17-II	35	3616.32	103.32	0.2126
W-4-16-II	133	13596.25	102.23	0.2103
N-4-13-II	31	3164.23	102.07	0.2100
W-4-12-II	21	2135.56	101.69	0.2092
W-1-12-II	37	3759.77	101.62	0.2091
M-4-12-I	79	7936.82	100.47	0.2067
W-1-12-III	9	894.23	99.36	0.2044
U-1-30-I	15	1468.27	97.88	0.2014
U-4-13-II	33	3208.89	97.24	0.2000
U-4-13-I	66	6342.50	96.10	0.1977
D-4-13-I	48	4581.30	95.44	0.1964
G-4-22-I	42	3961.51	94.32	0.1940
D-1-20-I	16	1508.77	94.30	0.1940
K-1-50-I	71	6673.70	94.00	0.1934
G-1-20-II	7	657.29	93.90	0.1932
N-1-30-I	14	1314.08	93.86	0.1931
K-1-13-I	154	14416.21	93.61	0.1926
U-1-14-I	30	2799.78	93.33	0.1920
G-1-12-II	6	556.74	92.79	0.1909
M-4-21-I	25	2284.23	91.37	0.1880
W-1-20-I	89	8095.03	90.96	0.1871
I-4-19-I	16	1446.34	90.40	0.1860
K-4-18-I	128	11559.53	90.31	0.1858
W-1-30-I	44	3952.12	89.82	0.1848
G-4-13-I	21	1861.73	88.65	0.1824
G-4-23-I	7	608.01	86.86	0.1787
I-1-30-I	8	693.53	86.69	0.1783
K-1-14-II	14	1211.52	86.54	0.1780
L-4-13-I	85	7323.16	86.15	0.1772
E-4-11-I	30	2551.40	85.05	0.1750
O-6-10-I	256	20909.17	81.68	0.1680

MY-DRG	No. of Episodes Per DRG	Total Pharmacy Cost per DRG	Average Pharmacy Cost per DRG	Pharmacy Service Weight
M-1-50-II	10	813.36	81.34	0.1673
M-4-11-I	8	648.07	81.01	0.1667
J-4-20-I	13	1044.55	80.35	0.1653
W-4-13-II	9	722.97	80.33	0.1653
K-1-12-I	18	1442.13	80.12	0.1648
G-1-20-I	20	1597.57	79.88	0.1643
U-1-13-I	9	715.99	79.55	0.1637
W-1-11-II	20	1586.34	79.32	0.1632
O-6-11-II	10	793.13	79.31	0.1632
B-1-14-I	36	2828.96	78.58	0.1617
E-1-20-I	35	2742.63	78.36	0.1612
G-1-12-I	14	1093.44	78.10	0.1607
L-4-14-I	43	3349.93	77.91	0.1603
H-1-20-I	41	3172.61	77.38	0.1592
M-4-12-II	19	1445.85	76.10	0.1566
H-1-30-I	229	17271.23	75.42	0.1552
O-6-12-II	299	22486.94	75.21	0.1547
W-1-13-I	8	600.19	75.02	0.1543
G-4-16-II	11	825.14	75.01	0.1543
U-1-15-I	87	6437.99	74.00	0.1522
J-1-20-I	7	517.89	73.98	0.1522
U-4-14-II	20	1472.37	73.62	0.1515
V-1-13-I	29	2128.60	73.40	0.1510
N-4-13-I	36	2632.61	73.13	0.1504
O-6-13-II	270	19446.87	72.03	0.1482
F-4-14-I	16	1148.87	71.80	0.1477
H-1-30-III	5	357.39	71.48	0.1470
U-4-15-I	58	4097.40	70.64	0.1453
N-4-16-I	23	1616.30	70.27	0.1446
J-4-13-II	7	491.24	70.18	0.1444
G-4-26-I	37	2556.20	69.09	0.1421
V-4-11-I	32	2210.51	69.08	0.1421

MY-DRG	No. of Episodes Per DRG	Total Pharmacy Cost per DRG	Average Pharmacy Cost per DRG	Pharmacy Service Weight
O-6-12-I	671	46250.26	68.93	0.1418
W-1-12-I	52	3581.23	68.87	0.1417
A-4-13-II	90	6159.90	68.44	0.1408
T-4-11-I	6	395.02	65.84	0.1354
W-1-30-III	6	390.64	65.11	0.1339
W-4-16-I	253	16385.81	64.77	0.1332
A-4-13-I	43	2771.38	64.45	0.1326
V-1-12-I	11	695.70	63.25	0.1301
M-4-20-I	20	1245.63	62.28	0.1281
O-6-13-I	688	41889.99	60.89	0.1253
N-1-12-II	9	537.20	59.69	0.1228
N-4-15-II	7	413.81	59.12	0.1216
G-4-25-II	10	590.08	59.01	0.1214
G-4-24-I	42	2439.90	58.09	0.1195
N-4-15-I	15	859.26	57.28	0.1178
W-4-14-I	39	2181.90	55.95	0.1151
V-1-11-I	7	371.15	53.02	0.1091
U-4-14-I	80	4207.47	52.59	0.1082
A-4-12-I	7	363.18	51.88	0.1067
I-4-17-I	9	448.96	49.88	0.1026
W-4-14-II	40	1964.24	49.11	0.1010
N-1-12-I	11	527.88	47.99	0.0987
U-4-11-I	8	372.16	46.52	0.0957
A-4-12-II	7	321.54	45.93	0.0945
J-4-13-I	5	228.51	45.70	0.0940
G-4-16-I	7	313.50	44.79	0.0921
W-4-15-I	11	473.64	43.06	0.0886
U-4-12-I	6	231.91	38.65	0.0795
K-1-14-I	54	1942.32	35.97	0.0740
W-1-11-I	141	4426.79	31.40	0.0646
K-4-17-I	117	3625.94	30.99	0.0638
G-4-25-I	18	533.33	29.63	0.0610
W-4-13-I	23	637.16	27.70	0.0570
V-1-15-I	25	438.28	17.53	0.0361

www.ingramcontent.com/pod-product-compliance
Lightning Source LLC
Chambersburg PA
CBHW030752180526
45163CB00003B/996